THE ONLY TECHNICAL ANALYSIS BOOK YOU WILL EVER NEED

A Must-Have Charting Manual
for Traders and Investors

BY BRIAN HALE

Contents

INTRODUCTION

"Entry and exit points are vital parts of trading and investing. That is worth repeating. Entry and Exit points are vital parts of Trading and Investing whether you are Day Trading, Swing Trading, or a Long Term Investor. Why would you ever buy a stock at the wrong time? Unfortunately, many market participants with no training do it every day."
— Fred McAllen

Of course, the stock market goes up and down daily, and people make daily profits. But sadly, recent studies have confirmed that 70% to 80% of traders and retail investors lose money.

They would buy a stock when they see or hear a piece of good news that originally didn't seem valid at all, only to see the stock price shoot down. And this is why most people find the stock market very confusing and illogical. In fact, some people believe that winning in the stock market is simply a game of chance.

So yes, while the stock market can be a complex and unpredictable world where traders and investors can make or lose large amounts of money quickly, the reality is that several factors can contribute to losses in the stock market.

You don't have to blame the market or call trading gambling. Instead, you should examine the underlying reasons for your losses.

Fear of losing money due to poor investment decisions can lead investors to make impulsive trades or avoid certain investments altogether, resulting in missed opportunities or significant losses. Economic instability, including recessions or market crashes, can also significantly impact the value of stocks and other investments.

For many investors, their financial future is at stake in the stock market, which can lead to a sense of desperation or panic when losses occur. Market volatility, which refers to the degree of fluctuation in the stock market, can also contribute to losses, particularly for traders and investors who are not well-informed or experienced.

Ultimately, the key to avoiding losses in the stock market is knowledge and applying careful analysis. You need to research stocks, understand market trends and patterns, and make rational decisions based on data rather than emotions to navigate the complexities of the stock market and achieve your financial goals.

So, if you've been thinking and asking yourself questions like:

"How can I earn a consistent income from the stock market?"

"What stocks should I trade that will yield the best return for me?"

"How do I know when to enter and exit a trade?"

"What's the holy-grail strategy famous traders, investors, and financial gurus like George Soros, Ray Dalio, Warren Buffett, etc., use to make a fortune in the markets?"

Rest assured that you will have answers to all your questions when you read this book. Your trading journey is about to take a turn for the better as you will discover winning trading techniques you can easily use to make money in the stock market. Moreover, these strategies will work regardless of whether the stock market is going up or down.

Before we proceed, I must tell you about myself so you understand why you should listen to me and do what I say. My name is Brian Hale, and I'm a self-described "nerd" who loves technical analysis and the stock market to the core. I have garnered several years of experience swing trading the stock market. I have achieved impressive returns on investments and my overall success in the financial market today because I have developed a deep understanding of market trends and patterns.

I believe that everyone has the potential to be a successful trader and investor if they have the right tools and information. And I'm passionate about empowering others to achieve their financial goals using technical analysis to trade the stock market.

Technical analysis is an effective method of predicting the short-term movements of stocks.

But what makes it so successful?

The reason is simple: we humans are emotional beings.

In an ideal world, stocks would be trading at their fair market value, which would be based solely on their fundamentals. Whenever a company announces its earnings, the stock price adjusts accordingly to reflect its fair value.

However, in reality, we do not live in a perfect world, and supply and demand, driven by emotions, are factors that influence stock prices.

For instance, when people hear a rumor about a company being better than others, they buy the stock, causing its price to trend upwards, and others will follow suit, leading to even higher prices. Conversely, when a stock price falls, people become fearful and start to sell their shares, causing further panic and even lower prices.

Technical analysis, also known as price action, considers these emotional factors, explaining why stocks can stay overvalued or undervalued for extended periods. It also acknowledges that, in the short term, stocks can disregard fundamentals and follow technology trends.

Small things could be extremely significant when performing thousands of operations through a microscope. As a result, I analyze charts bar by bar to glean any relevant information that each bar may reveal. However, at the end of each bar, most traders are often confused about what occurred and choose to wait for a pattern they recognize instead of analyzing it. They may dismiss it as institutional program activity, which they believe is not tradable by an individual trader. Though these instances constitute the vast minority of the day, traders do not feel involved in the market at such times.

Nonetheless, by examining certain factors like the volume, traders can see that the ignored bars have just as much volume as the bars they use for their trades. Many trades occur during such times, but traders do not understand how this can happen and pretend it does not exist.

Denying the reality of ongoing trading can be detrimental, as you, as a trader, owe it to yourself to understand when a trade is happening and develop strategies to profit from it. Although learning what the market reveals is challenging and time-consuming, it provides the foundation for successful trading.

My goals for writing this book are to describe my understanding of why specific trades trend the way they do, offer great risk-reward ratios, and present ways to profit from certain setups in stock trading.

The most important tip I can give you is to focus on the best deals, avoid the worst settings, and work on increasing the number of shares you trade. My reasons for sharing each approach or technique are merely my opinion and my logic for why a trade works may be utterly incorrect. That is, however, irrelevant. What matters is that reading price action is an effective approach to trade, and I'll go into great detail about why certain things happen the way they do. My explanations are backed by real world experience, and they offer me confidence when I place a trade.

The Only Technical Analysis Book You Will Ever Need is a comprehensive guide to understanding price action and is directed toward beginners, sophisticated traders, and market professionals. The concepts are useful to traders at all levels. It explores many standard techniques renowned traders and investors use but will focus more on everything you can find on the trading chart.

Most books point out three or four trades on a chart, which implies that everything else on the chart is incomprehensible, meaningless, or risky. I believe that there is something to be learned from every tick that takes place during the day and that there are far more great trades on every chart than just a few obvious ones, but to see them, you have to understand price action. You cannot dismiss any information on the chart as unimportant.

Unlike most books on candle charts, where a minority of readers feel compelled to memorize patterns, this book will explain why particular patterns are reliable setups for traders.

In the end, you'll:

- Acquire the right knowledge about technical analysis, including learning to read and analyze trading charts;

- Learn about the most common reasons why beginner investors and traders lose money in stocks;

- Identify chart patterns and trends and make better trading decisions as a result;

- Understand simple candlestick patterns you can use to find trading opportunities no matter which way the market is moving;

- Know how to aim for a better risk-to-reward ratio—this will change your trading game forever;

- Learn about the key technical indicators you need to milk the stock market;

- Be able to discipline yourself and do away with emotions when trading the stock market;

- Overcome the fear of making mistakes and losing money; and,

- Improve your investment skills and increase your chances of success and making profits and much more.

Once you understand the concepts in this book, you will be surprised to see how easy it is to understand how the stock market moves and how to manage your money so that you cut your losing stocks early and hold on to your winning stocks. That way, you'll become one of the top 10% of the successful traders in the stock market who make almost all the money. And in no time, you'll be on the path to building wealth and retiring early.

As we proceed to the first chapter, I advise you to prepare yourself because making a change requires deliberate effort. You'll have to take action and put in the work to get the result you want.

So, are you ready?

Well, then, let's dive in!

Chapter 1

Mastering the Market

"An investment in knowledge pays the best interest."
— *Benjamin Franklin*

In the 1950s, William O'Neil started as a stockbroker in Los Angeles, where he noticed a pattern among successful investors: they all used fundamental analysis to pick stocks.

However, O'Neil also realized that fundamental analysis alone wasn't enough to make consistent profits in the stock market. He studied successful stocks' price and volume patterns and started incorporating technical analysis into his investment strategy.

One day, O'Neil stumbled upon a stock called Teledyne, trading at $16 a share. After analyzing the stock's chart, he noticed that Teledyne had all the characteristics of a big winner:

- It was breaking out of a long consolidation period.

- Its earnings were strong.

- Its management team was top-notch.

O'Neil bought the stock and watched it rise to $100 a share over the next few years.

Using the experience gained from that event, O'Neil developed his CAN SLIM investing system, which combines fundamental and technical analysis to identify winning stocks. CAN SLIM stands for **C**urrent earnings, **A**nnual earnings, **N**ew products or services, **S**upply and demand, **L**eader or laggard, **I**nstitutional sponsorship, and **M**arket direction.

Many investors have praised O'Neil's emphasis on technical analysis in his CAN SLIM system, as it allows traders to identify stocks exhibiting strong price and volume patterns. Today, the CAN SLIM system is widely used by investors worldwide, and William O'Neil is recognized as one of the most successful investors ever.

Using technical analysis, you, too, can up your trading and investing game as it provides you with a framework to analyze price trends, patterns, and other market data. This will enable you to make more informed decisions about when to buy, sell, or hold your investments. And that's why I want us to start this book by exploring in great detail what technical analysis is and why it works.

Technical Analysis is Your Key to Trading Success

Technical analysis is a strategy that uses past prices and volume data to anticipate future price movements of securities. Rather than assessing a security's intrinsic value, a technical analyst relies on charts, indicators, patterns, and other tools to identify trends and predict future market activity. It is a graphical representation of a market's past and present performance. It enables traders to utilize the information in price action, patterns, and indicators to anticipate future trends and make informed trading decisions.

At its core, technical analysis aims to understand supply and demand in the market to determine the likely direction or trend of security, enabling traders to make buy or sell decisions accordingly.

According to the theory behind technical analysis, the market participants' collective actions reflect all the relevant information regarding security and assign a fair market value to it. Instead of analyzing the individual components of a security, technical analysis seeks to understand the emotions of the market by studying the market itself.

Understanding the benefits and limitations of technical analysis can provide traders and investors with a new set of tools to make better investment decisions. It is an important tool in a trader's toolkit as it provides a data-driven approach to evaluating securities. Technical analysis can be used with fundamental analysis to provide a more comprehensive view of the market, although it relies little on fundamental analysis. Economic indicators are already included in the market's activity in some way for technical analysts.

Technical analysis gives traders quick and easy access to a snapshot of relevant data, including price movement, volume, and open interest, all presented in one chart. This means you don't need to wait for monthly or quarterly data releases or seasonal events to make decisions about entering the market.

Using the right analysis tools, traders can quickly determine whether a trade is worth entering, estimate profit targets, and set risk management parameters. This makes technical analysis a more efficient and lower-risk alternative to pure fundamental analysis, which involves greater exposure to risk.

Of course, technical analysis is not perfect, and it has flaws. For example, it depends entirely on market participants' activities (individuals or entities that buy and sell securities).

As a result, you'll need to learn how to understand the calculations or information obtained from the chart better than the others. While the numbers themselves accurately compute deviation, relative strength, and so on, how these data are interpreted is important. As you will see in the following chapters, there is no wrong way to read the gathered data, but there is a better method.

How Technical Analysis can Revolutionize Your Trading Game

Technical analysis will help you understand herd psychology and market trends. Its beauty lies in the fact that it allows traders to interpret charts better to understand investors' moods towards a particular company or industry. For example, a strong upward movement in a share price typically indicates optimism and excitement among investors, while a downward trend may reflect pessimism and pressure on sellers.

After reading about it in this book, let's say you decide to try out technical analysis. But before now, you've been relying on your intuition and fundamental analysis to make your trades, but you are intrigued by using objective data to make more informed decisions.

So you start to study charts and use various indicators to analyze price and volume movements. You can identify trends and patterns you've previously missed and feel more confident in your trades.

Then one day, you notice a stock trending downward for weeks. While fundamental analysis would lead you to believe the stock is a good buy based on its low price-to-earnings ratio, the technical analysis shows it is in a strong downtrend with no signs of reversal.

So you decide to stay out of the trade, and within a few days, the stock plummeted further, confirming your analysis. And that's it! Thanks to your use of technical analysis, you've avoided a potentially costly mistake and revolutionized your trading game. This tells you how powerful technical tool analysis can be and the wonders it can do for your trading activities.

With the right tools and knowledge, you can use technical analysis to make more informed trading decisions and increase your chances of market success. Let's check out how technical analysis can help you make better trades.

Objective Analysis

Technical analysis relies on objective data, such as price and volume, which can be analyzed using various tools and indicators. This approach is more objective than fundamental analysis, which relies on subjective interpretations of financial statements and economic data.

By focusing on the price chart, technical analysis allows traders to track the movements of an asset and identify trends, support and resistance levels, and potential trade opportunities. This approach is particularly useful for short-term traders who must make quick decisions based on changing market conditions.

Historical Data

Technical analysis uses historical data to identify trends and patterns, which can provide insights into market behavior and help traders anticipate future market movements. By analyzing past market data, you can uncover common patterns and use them to make trading decisions. These patterns may include chart patterns such as triangles or head and shoulders, and indicators, such as moving averages or oscillators.

While it's important to note that history doesn't repeat itself, you must understand that human psychology and market behavior tend to follow certain patterns over time. Traders and investors are driven by emotions such as fear and greed, which can create predictable patterns in asset prices across different time frames.

You can gain an edge in the market by recognizing and using these patterns to guide your trading decisions. You should use historical data as a guide and the current price action as a catalyst, while looking for opportunities to buy or sell based on your market trends and patterns analysis. Ultimately, technical analysis aims to identify profitable trading opportunities by using objective data and historical patterns to anticipate future market movements.

Versatility

You can apply technical analysis to various securities, including stocks, bonds, currencies, and commodities. This is because the underlying principles of technical analysis are based on patterns of human behavior, which are universal across markets.

Traders who have mastered technical analysis can apply their knowledge to multiple markets, using price charts to identify patterns and make trading decisions. Technical analysis knowledge can be particularly useful when trading leveraged markets like forex, where movements can be amplified.

Moreover, technical analysis can be applied to any time frame, from minute-by-minute charts to daily or weekly charts. This is because financial markets exhibit fractal patterns, meaning that patterns observed in a one-time frame can also be observed in another. As a result, technical analysis can be used to identify short-term and long-term trends.

Risk Management

By identifying key support and resistance levels, you can determine potential entry points for your trades and set profit targets based on your risk tolerance and investment goals. For example, if a stock has been trading within a certain range for an extended period, you may buy when the price approaches the bottom and sell when it approaches the top.

Technical analysis can also provide early signals of potential trend reversals, allowing you to decide what to do with your active trades before the market moves against them. By analyzing market trends and patterns, you can identify potential support and resistance areas and set stop-loss orders to limit losses in case the market moves against them.

Why Technical Analysis is Only one Piece of the Trading Puzzle

When trading the stock market using technical analysis, I realized that although I was profitable, it wasn't only because of it. This initial understanding forced me to look critically at technical analysis to separate truth from hype.

I know many hard-core technical analysts would find what I'm saying surprising, but technical analysis has its place. Still, it's not how most traders and investors I have come across utilize it.

The Past Does not Equal the Future.

It's worth noting that past performance does not guarantee future results, and past performance may not be a reliable indicator of future results.

What do I mean?

The SEC requires that every investment include the disclaimer that past performance does not guarantee future outcomes. While this appears to be a straightforward statement, technical analysts say otherwise. By using charts, you may forecast future prices by using historical prices.

Remember that no matter how fast your chart is, it can only display prices from the past. The past cannot be exchanged. The SEC recognizes this and attempts to warn investors, but most do not listen. This is due to hindsight bias, which is a separate issue.

Hindsight Bias

The human inclination to project the past into the future is known as hindsight bias. You are guilty of hindsight bias if you glanced at a chart and thought, "If only I had bought here and sold there, I would have made a fortune."

Also, part of hindsight bias is how charts make investing appear simple (buy the lows, sell the highs). To be a good investor, you must control this misconception.

Subjectivity

Technical analysis is not an exact science, as it involves the subjective interpretation of data. Due to this, different traders may interpret the same data in different ways, leading to conflicting trading decisions.

To interpret charts, you need to have the right tools and skills. However, the interpretation of charts is very personal, similar to abstract art. Just like an abstract painting can be interpreted in many ways by different people, different chartists can interpret a set of chart figures differently.

The issue with most chart patterns is that they cause traders to change their opinion frequently, leading to constant changes in their trading decisions. Most chart services change their signals often, which results in their clients being pushed in and out of the market multiple times, benefitting the brokers' commissions but not the traders and investors.

Time-Consuming

Traders must dedicate significant time to analyzing historical data, studying charts, and using various tools and indicators to identify trends and patterns. Technical analysis requires considerable effort, especially for novice traders still learning to interpret charts and use technical indicators effectively.

This time-consuming aspect of technical analysis can be a significant disadvantage for traders who do not have the time or resources to devote to it. Many traders have other commitments and may not be able to dedicate enough time to analyze the market comprehensively. For instance, if you've got a full-time job, you may find monitoring the markets during working hours difficult. This can limit your ability to effectively use technical analysis, as you may miss out on key market developments and opportunities.

False Signals

Technical analysis can produce false signals due to its rigid approach to trading. Technical indicators generate buy and sell signals based on past market activity, and they do so regardless of the current market conditions. This can lead to false signals when market conditions are not ideal.

For instance, a stock may appear to be trending upward based on technical analysis, but it could be on the brink of a significant correction or reversal. This is because technical analysis does not consider external factors that can impact a security's performance, such as changes in the broader economy, regulatory shifts, or news events.

As such, traders relying solely on technical analysis may risk making trading decisions based on false signals, leading to losses instead of profits.

In the end, while technical analysis can provide traders with helpful information about a security's performance, it is important to remember that it is not foolproof.

Yes, technical analysis provides a large basket of tools and concepts for trading. Some successful traders use it and believe it is the best trading method. But ultimately, it is up to you to explore technical analysis and determine if it is right for you.

I recommend that traders and investors use technical analysis in conjunction with other forms of analysis and exercise caution and risk management when making trading decisions. That way, you will have a high chance of succeeding in trading.

The Technical Signal That Predicted the 2008 Great Recession

One of the most notable technical signals that predicted the 2008 Great Recession was the "inverted yield curve".

First, let's talk about the "yield curve".

The yield curve represents the bond market that displays the potential interest earnings for various maturities of bonds, and it is subject to change depending on economic activity.

Basic interest rate fundamentals must be reviewed to understand why the yield curve is such an efficient predictor of recessions.

The yield curve charts the interest rate yields of different debt instruments with varying maturities while keeping factors such as risk, liquidity, and tax treatment, constant. In the U.S., this curve is usually created for Treasury securities, and it typically slopes upward, indicating that longer-term Treasury securities have higher yields than shorter-term ones.

In case you're wondering what determines the yield curve's slope, it's the "expectations theory". And it claims that the link between yields and maturity, and consequently the slope of the curve, is explained by expectations about future interest rates. The theory suggests that investors are indifferent to the maturity of the instruments and only care about the expected returns. As a result, they will buy and sell products of varying maturities until long-term rates reflect an average of future short-term rates.

For instance, if a one-year bond pays 5% today, and a similar bond is expected to pay 7% in one year, an investor with a two-year investment horizon has different choices. They could buy a one-year bond today and another one, a year later, earning a 6% return if the expected rate materializes. Alternatively, the investor could buy a two-year bond today and keep it until it matures.

To determine the minimum annual yield required for the two-year bond to be as attractive as the first option, it must provide at least a 6% yield. If it earns less, investors will sell it, driving down the price and pushing the yield until it reaches 6%, the same as investing in two consecutive one-year bonds. This means that a two-year bond with a 6% yield reflects the market's expectation that the interest rate for a one-year bond one year from now will be 7%.

While the expectations theory cannot explain why the yield curve generally slopes upwardas it assumes that long-term rates would only exceed short-term rates if markets expect rates to rise in the future, which seems implausible—the evidence shows that investors expect rates to fluctuate equally between going up and down. This means that some expectations theory modification is necessary, and this is provided by the "preferred habitat theory".

This theory posits that the interest rate of a long-term bond will be equal to the average of the short-term interest rates expected during the bond's lifespan, plus a term premium. This premium is demanded by risk-averse investors who want to avoid potential significant capital losses on long-term debt.

This is because changes in interest rates can cause more significant fluctuations in the price of long-term bonds than in short-term bonds. For example, suppose the current rate of a one-year bond is 10%. In that case, the anticipated rate for one-year bonds in one year is 14%, and investors require a term premium of 1% to invest in two-year bonds; the current rate of two-year bonds should be 13% according to the preferred habitat theory.

Now the question is, how does the yield curve forecast recessions?

Although term premiums vary over time, changes in market expectations of future short-term interest rates are the key drivers of day-to-day yield curve movements. A steep yield curve, where long-term rates are higher than short-term rates, often indicates anticipation of higher future short-term rates, whereas a flat curve suggests expectations of falling short-term rates.

Expectations of future interest rates are based on economic activity and monetary policy expectations. For example, short-term rates usually decrease during a recession as the demand for credit drops and the Federal Reserve loosens monetary policy. If investors predict a recession, they will expect short-term rates to decline. This decline could lead to an inverted yield curve if it is significant enough to offset the term premium.

In essence, an inverted yield curve occurs when the yields on shorter-term bonds are higher than those on longer-term bonds, resulting in an upside-down curve on a graph plotting yield versus maturity.

Historically, many experts consider the inverted yield curve to be one of the most reliable indicators of a recession, and it has historically been accurate in predicting several economic downturns. In contrast, long-term investments, which typically have lower yields, are perceived as being less risky.

Since 1960, an inverted yield curve has preceded all five recessions. An inverted yield curve has been viewed as a warning sign for an upcoming recession. It indicates that investors are demanding higher yields for short-term investments due to perceived economic risks in the near future.

The yield curve began to invert in 2005, with the spread between the 2-year and 10-year Treasury yields falling dramatically. This pattern persisted into 2006 and 2007, with the yield curve entirely inverting several months before the recession began in December.

In the case of the 2008 Great Recession, the inverted yield curve was a warning indication that the economy was on the verge of a catastrophic disaster, and traders and investors who heeded this signal were likely able to mitigate their losses.

In 2022, the yield curve inverted, and this trend is expected to continue in 2023. When comparing two important indicator rates along the curve—the 2-year Treasury note and the 10-year Treasury note—the yield curve first inverted on April 1, 2022. After a brief period, rates returned to normal, but an inversion between 2-year and 10-year Treasuries occurred again in early July. The short-term 3-month Treasury bill yield surpassed the 10-year Treasury note in late October. The spread grew in the first months of 2023 as the inversion got more pronounced around the end of 2022. Interest rates on 3-month Treasury bills are approximately 1% higher than on 10-year Treasury bonds.

The 3-month Treasury bill yielded 4.88% at the end of February 2023, while the 2-year Treasury note yielded 4.81%. In comparison, the 10-year U.S. Treasury note yield was 3.92%.

Some analysts view this unusual occurrence as a major economic indicator, with many predicting that it portends a future recession. Attached is a chart showing the inverted yield curve obtained from one of the following sources, which predicts another likely recession:

Most Inverted in Decades
Treasury yield curve move extended after Fed decision

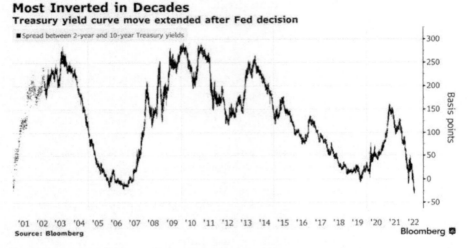

Source: Bloomberg

Typically, the inverted yield curve can be a leading signal of economic weakness or recession, but they are also an early warning sign.

As we round off this chapter, I must reiterate that no system or algorithm can confidently anticipate future share price movements based on the past. While analyzing charts can help you better understand when it is a good time to open or close a trade, it is not infallible, and it is crucial to be aware of its limitations. Essentially, even if all indicators converge to offer you purchase signals, the share price could continue to decrease.

So as a smart trader or investor, you want to make sure you combine technical analysis with another form of analysis, such as fundamental analysis, before deciding to buy or sell a security.

Now that you know why technical analysis helps you become a profitable trader and investor, it's time to advance our lessons. The next chapter will examine what elements and tools technical analysis uses to identify buying and selling points.

Key Takeaways

- Technical analysis is a strategy that uses past prices and volume data to anticipate future price movements of securities.

- You can up your trading and investing game using technical analysis as it provides a framework to analyze price trends, patterns, and other market data.

- Using the right analysis tools, traders can quickly determine whether a trade is worth entering, estimate profit targets, and set risk management parameters.

- As a smart trader or investor, you want to ensure you combine technical analysis with another form of analysis.

Unlocking the Secrets of the Markets

"The statement "market action discounts everything" forms what is probably the cornerstone of technical analysis. [...] The technician believes that anything that can possibly affect the price – fundamentally, politically, psychologically, or otherwise – is actually reflected in the price of that market."
— *John Murphy*

Buying and selling corporate securities has been studied thoroughly from various perspectives and by different individuals over the past century. The capital market offers immense rewards for those who make the right decisions and harsh penalties for those who are careless or unlucky.

As a result, the capital market has attracted some of the most intelligent accountants, analysts, researchers, and a mixed group of mystics, hunch players, and ordinary citizens with high hopes.

Intelligent minds have searched, and continue to search, for reliable methods of assessing the state and direction of the market, and identifying the appropriate security, such as stocks, bonds, currencies, etc., to purchase and the ideal time to purchase them. This thorough research has not been in vain. It has led to the development of technical analysis.

Like O'Neil, several successful traders and investors have credited technical analysis as the key to unlocking the market and achieving consistent returns. Through one means or another, they have gained the required understanding of the forces they are dealing with and have developed the ability to make wise decisions, exercise prudence and exercise crucial self-control to make profitable trading decisions. One example is Paul Tudor Jones, a billionaire hedge fund manager who has used technical analysis to achieve consistent returns over the years.

Jones, the founder of Tudor Investment Corporation, is one of the most successful traders ever. He is widely known for his prediction and profit from the 1987 stock market crash. Jones used technical analysis to identify an emerging bear market and took positions that would profit from the impending downturn. His trade earned him over $100 million and solidified his reputation as a legendary trader.

Renowned for his focus on macroeconomic trends and technical analysis to identify potential trading opportunities, Jones has used it to achieve consistent returns over the years. He has stated that "the basis of my trading is the use of technical analysis, and I've never seen anyone who has made money consistently over the long term without using it."

Therefore, it's important to take a closer look at technical analysis and observe its two key elements: a) support and resistance and volume; and, (b) the tools used to identify buying and selling points based on the key elements such as charts and technical indicators.

Support and Resistance

One of the most commonly used technical analysis techniques in the financial markets is support and resistance. Jones has used this approach to identify key support and resistance levels in markets such as gold and oil, allowing him to take profitable positions based on his analysis.

Support and resistance is a simple technique for quickly analyzing a chart to identify three points of interest to a trader. These are:

• The direction of the market.

• Potential levels at which the price of an asset may stop moving in a particular direction or reverse its direction.

• Establishing points to enter and exit the market.

If, as a trader, you can determine answers to these three points, then you can essentially have a trading idea.

By identifying levels of support and resistance on a chart, you can make informed trading decisions based on market sentiment and the potential for the market to breakout and continue in your expected direction or reverse and move in the opposite direction. Below is a pictorial illustration of what support and resistance looks like on the chart:

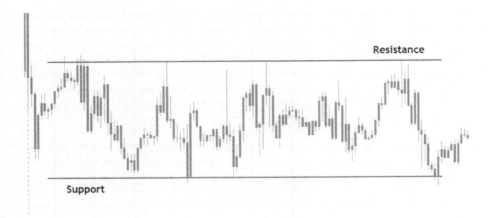

Support

The concept of support in trading refers to a specific area on a chart where the price has dropped to, but is having difficulty moving below. The chart given above illustrates that when the price reaches the support level, which is where buyers are likely to enter the market, it rebounds sharply from that point.

The fundamental idea behind the support level is that it is the price level at which the buying power or demand is strong enough to halt a further decline in the price.

As the price approaches the support level—a floor to prevent further price depreciation—and becomes cheaper, buyers consider it as an attractive opportunity and become more likely to buy. Conversely, sellers may be unwilling to sell the asset at lower prices as they are getting a worse deal. In such circumstances, the demand from buyers overcomes the supply from sellers, leading to the price being restricted from falling below the support level and reversing its direction to the upside.

Resistance

Resistance refers to an area on a chart where the price of an asset has risen to but is having difficulty moving above. The chart I've shared earlier also illustrates how the price rises up to the resistance level, which is where sellers are likely to enter the market, and subsequently experience a sharp decline.

In theory, resistance is the price level at which selling pressure (supply) is strong enough to hinder the price from rising any further. The reason behind this is that as the price moves closer to the resistance level and becomes increasingly expensive, sellers become more inclined to sell while buyers may be unwilling to continue buying the asset at higher prices. Consequently, selling pressure (supply) will exceed buying pressure (demand), preventing the price from exceeding the resistance level, and leading to a potential reversal in price direction to the downside.

Generally, support and resistance levels are identified beforehand. Identifying a support level implies finding a previous low. On the other hand, a resistance level is identified by a previous peak.

But one thing worth noting is that price will not respect support and resistance levels forever. This means that after support and resistance levels have held for a while, they will, at one point, break out to either the downside or upside, forming either a downtrend or an uptrend respectively. That way, the support level broken to the downside will become the new resistance, while the resistance level broken to the upside becomes the new support; a phenomenon technical analysts refer to as role reversal.

Let's say that the support level is at $100 for a certain stock. The traders who went long bought the stock at $100 and are happy to see it rise to $110. However, they wish they had bought more shares at $100. When the price drops to $100 again, they are likely to buy more shares to increase their position.

The traders who went short sold the stock at $100, hoping to profit from a price decline. However, they see the price rise to $110 and realize they may have made a mistake. They are now hoping for the price to drop back down to $100 so they can get out of their position without losing money.

The undecided traders have not made a decision on whether to go long or short on the stock. They see the price rise to $110 and realize that the trend is upward. They are waiting for a good opportunity to buy, which they believe will be when the price drops back down to $100.

If the price does drop back down to $100, all three groups will be interested in buying. The traders who went long will want to increase their position, the traders who went short will want to close their position, and the undecided traders will want to enter the market. This increase in buying pressure will cause the price to rise, and the $100 support level will become more significant as a result.

Over time, if the stock price continues to bounce off the $100 support level, more traders will become aware of its significance, and it will become a more established level of support. This is because traders would have seen that the stock price has consistently been supported at that level in the past, making it more likely that it will be supported at that level in the future.

The chart above shows a support that is violated. The support levels become resistance levels on subsequent bounces.

Now let's assume that prices move lower and break through the previous support level. Traders who bought at that level may panic and start selling to limit their losses. Those who went short will be pleased with their position and may hold onto it or even add to it. The undecided traders may become more bearish and start selling as well.

As a result, the support level will turn into a resistance level, where traders will sell at subsequent rallies or bounces. This is because the previous support level has now become a reference point for traders, and they will use it to make trading decisions in the future.

Bearing these factors in mind, we as traders need to adopt sound risk management to limit losses when such breakouts occur, and, if possible, take advantage of it. Of course, we will cover these in detail in subsequent chapters.

Volume

Trading volume reflects the overall activity of the market, indicating the sheer number of a security's shares traded during a given period. Next to price, it is one of the most closely watched indicators, and that's why it's a critical factor for buying and selling securities.

Trading volume also indicates the momentum of a security being traded, and so, it is an important technical indicator used by investors to confirm trends in price movements. Volume gives traders and investors an idea of the price action of a security and whether to buy or sell the security.

Increasing trading volume is generally associated with positive price movement, and vice versa. The trading volume serves as a warning as to whether a stock is on the verge of breaking into upside territory (high volume) or into a downside trend (low volume). High volume also gives investors more time to determine when it's the right time to sell for a profit.

So, for instance, if a stock is experiencing an uptrend in price and trading volume is increasing, this can confirm that the uptrend is strong and may continue. And if a stock is experiencing a downtrend in price and trading volume is decreasing, this can confirm that the downtrend is weak and may reverse.

Typically, high trading volume indicates that many investors are buying and selling shares, which can create liquidity and make it easier for traders to enter and exit positions. Stocks with high trading volume are relatively less volatile because price movements are smoother and more continuous, with a large number of transactions being executed. The stocks that are frequently bought and sold experience fewer sudden price changes. With many market participants buying and selling, and a large number of buy and sell orders being placed, the difference between the highest bid and the lowest ask prices is smaller, allowing the stock price to fluctuate in smaller increments. Furthermore, high-volume stocks respond less abruptly to news events compared to low-volume stocks. This is due to the efficiency of trading, as more market participants are involved in buying and selling the stock at any given time.

On the other hand, low trading volume can make it difficult for investors to find buyers or sellers for a particular stock. This can create liquidity issues and make it more challenging for traders to enter or exit positions. Low trading volume in a stock usually leads to higher volatility in the share price. The reason behind this is that with limited shares traded each day, the company's market value is calculated based on the most recent price per share, leading to large percentage fluctuations in market value on a daily basis. Additionally, because trades are infrequent and the number of shareholders is usually small in low-volume stocks, these stocks are more susceptible to price changes in response to news events.

In essence, high volume can also indicate that there are significant news or market events that are impacting the stock, which can create trading opportunities for investors who can interpret and act on the information.

Trading volume is a measure of the total number of shares of a particular security that are bought and sold during a specific period of time. It is not a calculated value but is instead determined by counting and reporting the actual number of shares traded. And I'll be showing you two indicators in particular that can help with that in the next chapter.

Charts

Chart reading is the single most important investing skill you'll ever learn. In fact, Jones has applied chart reading to great effect, using it to identify trends, potential reversals, and chart patterns that signal potential breakouts in markets such as bonds, currencies, and commodities.

Our goal is to use it to identify important price levels, such as support and resistance levels, and to track the strength of trends and momentum (velocity or speed at which the price changes). Technical analysts use charts to identify buying and selling opportunities to maximize profits.

Stock charts are highly valuable because they provide insight into the actions of large institutional investors, who account for the majority of trading activity in the market. These investors' buying and selling patterns can significantly impact stock prices.

As an individual investor, the goal is to invest in stocks that institutional investors are buying and avoid those that they are selling. Charts help achieve this goal by visually indicating when a stock is being bought or sold in large quantities, allowing investors to identify the best times to buy, sell, or hold their positions.

Charts tell a "story," and it is your responsibility to understand it. While some people regard charts as overly technical or a modern-day tea-leaf reading, a chart is simply a visual representation of changes in share price and trading activity.

Price movements over time are easily represented by charts. It depicts the trading activity that occurs during a particular trading period (whether that period is 5 minutes, 1 hour, 1 day, or 1 week). Any financial asset with market data over time can be used to create an analysis chart.

Price movements are a series of mostly random events, so as traders, our job is to manage risk and assess probability, and charting can help with that.

Charts are not mysterious or frightening in any way. This is particularly true when you consider that charts do only one thing: they tell you a story. They sift through all of the rumors, headlines, and hype to create a clear image of what is really going on with the stock.

By studying charts, you filter the noise in the market and easily identify trends and patterns in price movements and predict future price movements based on these patterns (we will study these patterns in detail in Chapter 6).

Analyzing stock charts allows you to create price charts for a specific company. Technical analysis is significant and can help draw attention to specific factors such as:

- More visibility on the fluctuations in the stock's price over time.

- Determining the stock's intrinsic value rather than its market value.

- Analyzing stock charts to evaluate the stock's overall performance in the market.

- Observe the impact of certain events on the stock's value before and after they occur.

- Easily identify persistent price fluctuations.

- Better understand trading levels and volume of trade for a particular stock.

- Increased ease at identifying support and resistance levels. With this information, investors can determine the optimal time to enter or invest in a particular stock, leading to higher returns on investment.

Finally, analyzing stock charts helps to identify prevailing market trends, including distinguishing between short-term and long-term trends, allowing for informed investment and trading decisions.

The candlestick chart is the most commonly used price chart by traders and investors. Other types include line chart, bar chart, Heikin Ashi, etc. Below is a picture that shows what a candlestick chart looks like:

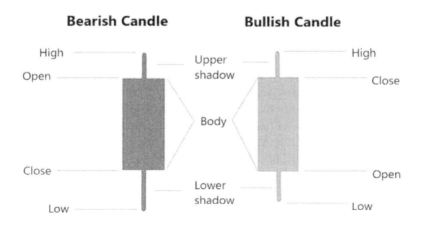

As you can see, with a vertical line, the candlestick bars above show the high-to-low range. The larger block (or body) in the center represents the price difference between the opening and ending prices. Candlesticks aid in visualizing bullish or bearish sentiment by displaying "bodies" in various hues.

In the example above, the darker color shows that the top of the candle block is the opening price, and the bottom of the candle block is the closing price. And that indicates the sellers were more than the buyers, and we call such a candle a bearish candle. Meanwhile, the lighter color shows that the bottom of the block is the opening price, and the top of the block is the closing price. And that indicates the buyers were more than the sellers, and we call such a candle a bullish candle.

A chart makes it simple to recognize and analyze the movements, structures, patterns, and tendencies of a currency pair. On the next page is an example of a 1-day timeframe candlestick chart for Apple stock (AAPL):

On the stock chart shown above, the y-axis represents the price of the stock and the x-axis represents the time period over which the price data is plotted. The time periods can vary depending on the chart type, but the most common time frames are daily, weekly, and monthly. The most recent price is plotted on the right-hand side of the chart, and the chart shows the price history of the stock over the selected time period.

Technical Indicators

Technical indicators are tools we use to determine future trends of a traded security during technical analysis. They help traders and investors make informed decisions on when to enter or exit a trade to make a profit. Even Jones uses technical indicators such as moving averages, oscillators, and momentum indicators to confirm his analysis and make informed trading decisions.

Technical indicators examine past trading data such as price, volume, and open interest rather than a company's fundamentals. They translate this data into simple, easy-to-read signals that help investors determine the correct time to buy or sell.

Technical indicators, such as trend indicators and oscillators are commonly used by active traders to analyze price movements, both for the short-term and long-term. The benefits of using technical indicators include the ability to identify market patterns, interpret future price behavior, and make educated investment decisions. The following are the several benefits of using technical indicators:

- Provides an overall view of the security's price action's strength and direction.

- Smooths out data and makes market prices easier to understand as they help in plotting the movements of the stock on a chart.

- Use for determining support and resistance levels.

- Helps traders identify potential buy and sell signals.

- Helps in establishing upward and downward trends. This is critical for both traders and investors.

- Alerts the technical analyst of any major price action or volatility.

- Provides insights into market behavior to make more informed trading decisions.

Now, in case you're wondering how technical indicators work, they are typically mathematically derived representations of data, such as price, volume, or open interest, used to identify stock movement. To evaluate investments and spot trading opportunities, technical indicators are weighted based on historically adjusted returns, common sense, an investor's goal, and logic.

Certain technical indicators generate signals independently, while others complement each other. Technical indicators are utilized in technical analysis to assess the strength or weakness of a security by examining trading signals, patterns, price movements, and various analytical charting tools. Although some technical indicators are applicable to any financial market, some are intended for use in a specific market.

Technical indicators are of two types: oscillators and overlays.

Oscillators

Oscillators, also known as leading or momentum indicators, are a type of technical indicators that fluctuate between a local minimum and maximum and are graphed above or below a price chart. Examples of oscillators include the stochastic oscillator, MACD, and RSI.

Oscillators are particularly useful in indicating overbought and oversold price movements. Traders and investors often use oscillators to identify price reversals within a range-bound market, as oscillators tend to oscillate within a generally defined range. However, it's worth noting that oscillators can sometimes give false signals during trending markets or volatile market conditions. The following are the benefits and drawbacks of oscillators:

- It aids in early entrance and exit signaling.

- These indicators produce more signals and provide increased trading opportunities.

- Early warning signs can point out possible strengths or weaknesses.

- The Technical analysis indicator is widely used in trading markets because leading indicators produce more calls.

- More signals and early signals indicate the possibility of false alarms.

- False signals raise the possibility of loss.

Overlays

Overlays are technical indicators that are plotted over the top of prices on a chart and are also known as lagging indicators. They use the same scale as prices, and examples include moving averages and Bollinger Bands. Traders and investors use overlays to identify the market direction and determine overbought and oversold levels. Overlays provide insight into the supply and demand of a traded security. The following are the benefits and drawbacks of overlays:

- It aids in early signaling for entry and departure.

- These indicators produce more signals and provide increased trading possibilities.

- Early warning signs can serve as a warning against a possible strength or weakness.

- Because leading indicators produce more calls, the Technical analysis indicator is widely used in trading markets.

- More signals and early signals indicate the possibility of false alarms.

- False signals raise the risk of loss.

Ultimately, your focus should be on price action—that is, studying chart patterns objectively and not solely relying on indicators, as they are merely derivatives and not a direct reflection of price action. In essence, you should use indicators only for confirmations.

Overlaying Technical Indicators on Charts for Maximum Effect

So earlier, we talked about overlay indicators, otherwise known as lagging indicators. In this section, I want us to take a closer look at them, especially how to use them to trade.

Overlay indicators are indicators that are put directly on the price portion of the candlestick chart. By superimposing them, the indicators become more aligned with the stock price, providing greater accuracy and ease. These indicators scale and adapt to the price chart, displaying important information such as visual trend direction, trading range, and support/resistance levels.

Below you can see the picture of the S&P 500 stock chart showing price action with candlesticks:

And below is another picture showing the same chart, but this time with a 50-day moving average technical overlay, signaling a change in direction of the market trend.

When analyzing an asset, traders frequently employ a plethora of technical indicators. With thousands of various options, you must select the indicators that works best for you and become familiar with how they operate. To generate trade ideas, you can also combine technical indicators with more subjective types of technical analysis, such as chart patterns.

But before we move on to a more in-depth look at charts and patterns, I want us to look at the different oscillators and overlays you can use for your trading and how they'll help you to confirm the entry and exit points you've identified on your charts before you make a final decision to buy or sell.

Key Takeaways

- Support and resistance is a strong trading pillar, and most strategies incorporate some form of support/resistance analysis.

- Price will not always heed support and resistance. Keeping this in mind, traders must use sensible risk management to limit losses if a breakout occurs.

- Volume gives traders and investors an idea of the price action of a security and whether to buy or sell the security.

- Charts are used to identify important price levels, such as support and resistance levels, and to track the strength of trends and momentum (velocity or speed at which the price changes).

- Technical indicators examine past trading data such as price, volume, and open interest rather than a company's fundamentals.

Navigating the Overlays

"You need a well-thought-out plan which anticipates all potential scenarios to keep you from making impulsive and emotional decisions during market hours. You are being bombarded constantly with new information from peers, television, price action, websites, etc. Trading stocks is a business, and if you want your business to thrive you must have a plan which you execute flawlessly."
— Brian Shannon

Another key function of technical analysis is its ability to identify trends, momentum, volatility, and volume in the market. By studying price and volume data, you can identify patterns that indicate the direction and strength of a trend. This will enable you to take positions that will profit from the trend and avoid positions that would be unprofitable in the current market environment.

George Soros is another billionaire investor who has greatly used this approach. Known for his focus on macroeconomic trends and ability to anticipate major market movements, Soros used technical analysis to identify long-term trends in markets such as currencies, commodities, and stocks and made profitable trades.

Soros established the Soros Fund, later known as Quantum Endowment Fund, in 1973. It was a hedge fund that created a range of associated companies. Although some of Soros's trades failed, his bold investment decisions caused the funds to grow rapidly. In October 1987, Soros accurately predicted the worldwide stock market crash, but he was wrong in his prediction that Japanese stocks would fall the hardest.

Soros gained almost mythical status in the financial world in September 1992 when the British government devalued the pound sterling. Through his Quantum group of companies, Soros had sold billions of pounds in the days preceding devaluation, most of which were purchased with borrowed money. Soros bought back pounds afterward, repaid the borrowed money, and profited approximately $1 billion. Although others also profited from the pound's fall,

Soros's operations were significantly larger than anyone else's, and he earned the moniker "the man who broke the Bank of England."

Today, Soros is among the wealthiest individuals globally, thanks to his investment success. He now uses some of his profits for philanthropy and has donated billions of dollars to various causes over the years.

In this chapter, we will explore how to study trends, momentum, volatility, and volume using technical indicators. Mind you, while there are several technical indicators out there, it's best to avoid using too many to avoid analysis paralysis, especially since these indicators essentially give you the same or very similar information. Based on experience, I will share the best two technical indicators you will need for each category.

Trend Indicators

Trend indicators are tools we use in technical analysis to identify the direction of the price movement of a financial asset over a given period of time. They help traders and investors to determine whether the price is moving up, down, or sideways. Here, we will focus on the two most popular and useful trend indicators:

Moving Averages

Moving averages (MA) are frequently used by a wide range of traders, but what makes them so popular, and what exactly are they? Well, let's see...

The moving average (MA) is a technical indicator used to identify or confirm the general trend, support, or resistance levels of asset prices. It calculates the average price of an asset over a given time period, and its purpose is to smooth out the price action—which can often be highly volatile and complex—into a clear and readable line that still indicates the overall direction of the asset's value.

The MA is updated regularly as new price data becomes available, and the calculation is straightforward. For example, a 50-day MA is calculated by adding the closing prices of the asset for the past 50 days and dividing that sum by 50.

Meanwhile, as each new day's closing price becomes available, the oldest price is dropped from the calculation, and the new one is added in, so the moving average "moves" forward in time.

There are different moving average indicators you can use, such as the 10-day moving average, the 15-day moving average, or the 40, or 100-day MA; but the longer the moving average's period, the more reliable it is. This means that a 200-day MA is considered more reliable than a 50-day MA.

However, traders often use multiple moving averages with different time periods, such as a 50-day (shorter-term) and a 200-day (longer-term) moving averages to identify potential areas of support and resistance, and trends. If the shorter-term moving average crosses above a longer-term moving average, it may be a bullish signal indicating that the asset's price is likely to continue rising. And if a shorter-term moving average crosses below a longer-term moving average, it may be a bearish signal indicating that the asset's price is likely to continue falling.

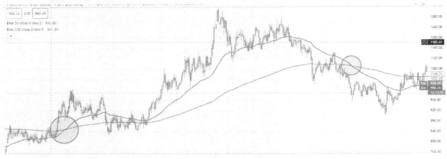

As you can see from the chart picture displayed above, moving averages can also provide buy and sell signals when they cross over one another. For clarification, when the price of the traded asset crossed above the 50-day and 200-day moving averages, you can see a clear uptrend which indicates a buying signal. Conversely, if the price crosses below the 50-day and 200-day moving averages, you can see a clear downtrend, which indicates a selling signal.

Price charts with moving average overlays work for a wide range of securities but are particularly helpful for securities that have high volatility and trading volumes, such as *Forex, commodities,* stocks, and cryptocurrencies.

Fibonacci Retracement

In trading, relying on intuition alone isn't enough. To reach success, traders utilize a variety of techniques and tools to forecast changes in asset prices, and one such tool is the Fibonacci retracement levels. These levels are represented by horizontal lines on a price chart that indicates potential support and resistance levels in price movement. This enables traders to determine the point at which the price may return to a previous level before resuming the trend.

The Fibonacci retracement tool is grounded on the belief that prices frequently retrace to a predictable portion of a move, after which they continue in the original direction. The concept of Fibonacci retracement is rooted in the work of Leonardo Fibonacci, a mathematician who lived during the 12th century.

We get the Fibonacci sequence of numbers from his efforts, as well as the well-known Fibonacci golden ratio. The Fibonacci sequence is a set of numbers in which the next number is merely the sum of the two numbers before it. For example, the sequence would be 0, 1, 1, 2, 3, 5, 8, 13, 21, 34, 55, 89, 144, and so on endlessly.

This sequence has been observed in many natural phenomena and is believed to have applications in financial markets. For example, dividing the number of female bees in a hive by the number of male bees yields the response 1.618. Each fresh sunflower seed is 0.618 of a turn away from the previous one. Fibonacci is also applicable to people. There are numerous examples of this golden ratio in action in our bodies, such as the length of your forearm to the length of your hand, which is 1.618.

But what makes the series so important for traders?

Well, it's because of the "Fibonacci's golden ratio," which is the ratio between the numbers in the series. If you observe closely, you will discover that any number divided by the preceding number yields 1.618 as we progress through the series. This is referred to as the "Fibonacci golden ratio."

The Fibonacci golden ratio in financial markets has the same mathematical foundation as the natural phenomena described above. When analysts use the golden ratio in technical analysis, the ratio is typically expressed as three percentages: 38.2% (often rounded to 38%), 50%, and 61.8% (often rounded to 62%). However, traders can use more multiples as needed, such as 23.6%, 161.8%, 423%, 684.4%, and so on.

Divide one number in the sequence by the number two places to the right to get the 38.2% ratio. 21 split by 55, for example, equals 0.382. The 23.6% ratio is calculated by dividing one number in the sequence by a number three places to the right. 8 split by 34, for example, equals 0.235. The Fibonacci retracement levels are made up of all of these values.

Assume a market has climbed and, like all markets, it does not move in a straight line and begins to decline. Traders will look at Fibonacci ratios to see where the decline will end, and the market will resume its prior rise.

Fibonacci retracement levels often identify retracement reversal marks with surprising accuracy. The retracement levels are a powerful instrument that can be applied to all timeframes, including day trading and long-term investing.

As a trader who wants to use the Fibonacci retracement tool, you first need to know the highest price point, usually referred to as the swing high, and lowest price point, usually referred to as the swing low of the asset.

Next, you draw horizontal lines at the key Fibonacci levels of 23.6%, 38.2%, 50%, 61.8%, and 100% between the swing high and swing low. Each level represents areas of support or resistance, with the 50% level being a neutral level. Luckily, many charting softwares have simplified the process of drawing Fibonacci lines; a good example is the TradingView charting tool.

The idea is that once the price bounces any of these levels, in the form of support or resistance, you can then decide whether to buy or sell the asset. I have provided a more detailed explanation using the chart attached on the next page.

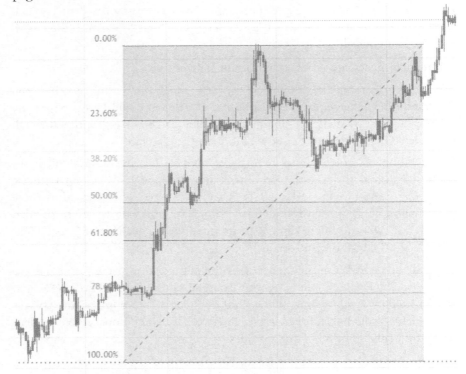

As you can see, the Fibonacci tool is drawn starting from the swing low up to the swing high, with different colors separating each retracement level. You can also see how the price retraced into the 38.2% level, signaling that the trend has paused and retraced, and a trader can possibly enter a new buy position.

This means that in an uptrend, you might consider going long (buy) on a retracement down to a key support level, whereas in a downtrend, you might consider going short (sell) when an asset retraces up to a key resistance level.

Fibonacci retracements are useful in securities that exhibit strong trends or are subject to price volatility. For example, they may be used in stocks that have recently experienced a sharp move in price or in currency pairs that tend to move in long-term trends.

Momentum Indicators (Oscillators)

Momentum indicators are technical analysis tools that measure the rate of change in a security's price over a given time period. Also known as oscillators, these tools create high and low bands between two extreme values before constructing a trend indicator that oscillates within these bounds.

Traders use oscillators to identify the strengths or weaknesses of a trend and to help traders make informed decisions about buying or selling a security. Let's check out the two most common ones.

Relative Strength Index (RSI)

J. Welles Wilder's Relative Strength Index (RSI) is a momentum oscillator that measures the speed and change of price movements and detects possible overbought or oversold conditions in a traded security. The RSI ranges from 0 to 100, and it is calculated by comparing the magnitude of an asset's recent gains to its recent losses.

The formula for calculating the relative strength index (RSI) is as follows:

Where:

RS is the average of x days' of upward price change divided by the average of x days' of downward price change.

The most usual time frame for calculating the RSI is 14 days, but this can be changed to meet the trader's needs.

When the RSI is plotted on a price chart, it typically appears as a line oscillating between 0 and 100. When the RSI is above 70, it is considered overbought, indicating that the asset's price may be due for a correction or a reversal. And when the RSI is below 30, it is considered oversold, indicating that the asset's price may be due for a bounce or a reversal.

These common levels can also be adjusted if required to better fit the security, particularly since the RSI may stay in an overbought or oversold zone for extended periods during strong trends. For example, if security is consistently hitting the overbought level of 70, you may want to raise it to 80 or 90.

The RSI tends to remain in the 40 to 90 range during an uptrend or bullish market, with the 40–50 zone serving as support, and it tends to stay between

10 and 60 during a downtrend or bearish market, with the 50–60 zone serving as resistance. These ranges will vary depending on the RSI settings and the strength of the security's or market's underlying tendency.

RSI also frequently creates chart patterns that may or may not be visible on the underlying price chart, such as double tops and bottoms and trendlines. Look for support or opposition on the RSI as well.

A phenomenon known as "divergence" may also occur on the RSI. It's a situation where the RSI and the price of the asset point in the opposite direction. For example, if the price of an asset is making higher highs while the RSI is making lower highs, this could be a sign of a low momentum, signaling a potential trend reversal.

The chart on the next page is a perfect example of this occurrence:

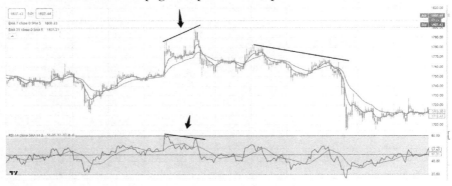

From the image above, you can see how price action showed a higher-high movement, while the RSI showed a lower-high movement in an overbought zone, confirming that the trend's momentum is possibly weak and is coming to an end. And eventually, the asset traded to the downside.

Securities that have a tendency to experience momentum and trending behavior, as well as those that are not highly volatile or subject to sudden price spikes or drops, can work well with the RSI indicator.

Stochastic Oscillator

The Stochastic Oscillator is a technical indicator that compares a security's most recent closing price to its price range over a set period of time, usually 14 periods. Similar to the RSI, it gives readings that move (oscillate) between 0 and 100 to provide an indication of the security's momentum.

The formula for calculating the Stochastic Oscillator is as follows:

$\%k =$

%D = 3-day SMA of %K

Where:

- C is the most recent ending price;

- Lowest Low is the time period's lowest low; and

- Highest High is the time period's highest high.

So, typically, the Stochastic Oscillator consists of two lines: the %K line and the %D line.

The %K line depicts the security's current price as a percentage of the price range over a given time period, while the %D line is a moving average of the %K line.

The following are the several uses of the stochastic oscillator:

- Used to identify overbought and oversold conditions in the market, as shown in the chart below.

- When the indicator crosses below 20, it is considered oversold, while a cross above 80 is considered overbought.

- Divergences between the Stochastic Oscillator and the price of the security can also provide other useful signals about trends. For example, if the price of a security is making higher highs, but the Stochastic Oscillator is making lower highs, it could be an indication that momentum is weakening, and a reversal could be imminent.

Traders can also use this oscillator in conjunction with other technical analysis tools, such as support and resistance and MAs, to confirm signals and identify potential trading opportunities. For example, in the chart below, the Stochastic Oscillator is indicating an oversold condition, while the price of a security is approaching a trendline below, signaling a potential buying opportunity.

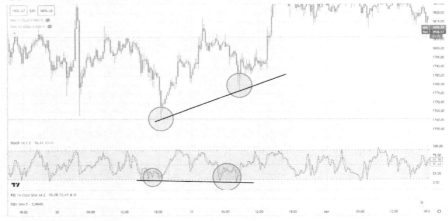

The Stochastic Oscillator is useful for securities that are subject to price volatility or that exhibit strong trends, as these conditions tend to create overbought and oversold conditions. For example, if a stock has been trading in a range for an extended period of time and then experiences a sharp price movement, the Stochastic Oscillator can help identify overbought or oversold conditions that may signal a potential reversal.

Volume Indicators

Volume indicators are technical analysis tools that use trading volume data to evaluate the strength or weakness of a market trend. They can provide useful information to traders about the buying and selling pressure of a particular asset or market, which can be used to make trading decisions. Again, we will examine only the two most common volume indicators used by traders.

On-Balance Volume (OBV)

The On-Balance Volume (OBV) is a technical indicator used to analyze the flow of money into and out of a security and to forecast changes in stock prices. It uses trading volume to determine market momentum. The creator of OBV, Joseph Granville, developed this metric in his book Granville's New Key to Stock Market Profits, which was published in 1963.

Granville believed that volume was the primary force behind market movements and designed OBV to predict when major market moves would occur based on volume changes. He believed that changes in volume occurred before price movements, and described OBV's forecasts as being like a tightly wound spring. Granville thought that when there is a significant increase in volume without a corresponding change in stock price, the stock's price would ultimately experience a sharp rise or fall.

The OBV line is formed by incorporating the volume on days when the price of the asset increases and subtracting the volume on days when the price decreases. Three guidelines are followed while computing the OBV:

- If the current day's closing price is greater than the previous day's closing price, then the present OBV is obtained by adding the current day's volume to the previous day's OBV.

- If the current day's closing price is less than the previous day's closing price, then the present OBV is calculated by subtracting the current day's volume from the previous day's OBV.

- If the current day's closing price is equal to the previous day's closing price, then the current OBV is equivalent to the previous day's OBV.

So what does the OBV indicator tell us?

Well, the theory is that if the price of a traded security goes up and the volume is higher than the previous day, then more money is flowing into the asset, and the OBV line goes up. Conversely, if the price goes down and the volume is higher than the previous day, then more money is flowing out of the asset, and the OBV line goes down.

Traders used the OBV indicator to confirm a price trend or to identify a divergence between the price and the volume. So, for example, if the price is going down, but the OBV line is going up, it could indicate that the price decrease is not supported by strong selling pressure, and a trend may be coming. Below is a perfect illustration of this occurrence:

In addition to using the OBV to predict price changes, technical analysts also use volume numbers to track large institutional investors. When there is a divergence between volume and price, it is seen as an indication of the relationship between institutional investors and individual investors. This can present opportunities for buying against incorrect prevailing trends. For instance, institutional investors may increase the price of an asset and then sell after other investors follow suit.

Stocks with high trading volumes and volatility are ideal for using OBV.

Volume RSI

The Volume RSI, also known as the Volume Relative Strength Index, is a technical indicator similar to the traditional RSI, but instead of using changes in price, it utilizes up-volume and down-volume in its formula. It combines price momentum with trading volume to provide a more complete picture of a security's trend strength. Traders use the Volume RSI to identify whether a security is experiencing a strong trend with high volume or a weak trend with low volume.

The traditional RSI only considers price movements and ignores the impact of volume on a security's trend. The volume RSI, on the other hand, incorporates trading volume into the RSI calculation. Yes, that's correct. While the price RSI measures the strength of up-moves and down-moves based on price changes, the Volume RSI indicator measures the strength of up-volume and down-volume by analyzing the amount of volume traded during those moves. This helps traders understand whether bullish or bearish money flow is stronger in a given period of time.

The volume RSI is calculated by dividing the cumulative volume of up days by the cumulative volume of down days over a specified time period. The resulting value is then plotted on a scale of 0 to 100, similar to the traditional RSI. This means that the Volume RSI oscillates in the range from 0 to 100.

The Volume RSI can be used to create trading signals by observing its crossovers with the 50% center-line that it oscillates around. The basic rules are as follows:

- When the Volume RSI crosses above the 50% level, it is considered a bullish signal, as the bullish volume is stronger than the bearish volume.

- Conversely, when the Volume RSI crosses below the 50% level, it is considered a bearish signal, as the bearish volume is stronger than the bullish volume.

As shown in the chart above, technical analysis would recommend using the following rules to generate buy/sell signals:

- You want to buy when the indicator moves above the 50% line after being below it;

- You want to sell when the indicator moves below the 50% line after being above it.

The Volume RSI is *u*seful for analyzing securities that are prone to price spikes or large swings in volume, *and p*articularly useful for analyzing stocks and ETFs that are actively traded with high volume.

And, of course, you can use the Volume RSI together with more than one indicator, such as the Moving Average, to confirm your entry and exit points. But as I mentioned at the beginning of this chapter, you shouldn't use too many indicators to avoid analysis paralysis; two or three indicators are okay.

Volatility Indicators

Volatility indicators are technical analysis tools that measure the degree of variation in a security's price over time. These indicators help traders determine the level of risk involved in a particular trade by identifying periods of high or low volatility. Here are some examples of commonly used volatility indicators:

Bollinger Bands

The Bollinger Bands measure the volatility of a traded security with the bands automatically widening when volatility increases and contracting when volatility decreases. Their dynamic nature allows them to be used on different securities with the standard settings.

47

Bollinger Bands are volatility bands that are positioned above and below a moving average and were invented by John Bollinger. The Bands consist of a set of three lines plotted on a price chart, usually using a moving average as a centerline and two additional lines plotted two standard deviations away from the centerline. These two additional plotted lines are referred to as the upper and lower bands of the indicator.

The upper Bollinger Band is calculated by adding two standard deviations to the moving average, while the lower Bollinger Band is calculated by subtracting two standard deviations from the moving average. This creates a channel or "band" around the moving average that widens or narrows based on the volatility of the asset's price movements.

The Bollinger Bands provide short-term traders with a tried-and-true instrument for developing trading strategies. Bollinger Bands can also be used by traders to:

• Determine high and low volatility times using the distance between bands;

• Determine whether the price movement is ranging or trending;

• Determine the likely peak and low prices for currency pairs;

• Aid in pattern identification;

• Examine price action in relation to different technical indicators;

• Make trading signs; and

• Identify overbought and oversold circumstances.

Typically, when the price moves above the upper band, it may be overbought, indicating a potential sell signal. Likewise, when the price moves below the lower band, it may be oversold, indicating a potential buy signal.

Below is a chart of what Bollinger Bands look like, with the circled areas showing the overbought and oversold zones of the traded asset:

Bollinger band overlays work well with price charts for stocks, exchange-traded funds (ETFs), futures contracts, currencies, and options. They work best with securities that tend to experience frequent and significant price movements (volatility).

Average True Range Indicator (ATR)

Average True Range (ATR) refers to a technical analysis indicator that measures volatility by taking into account the range of price movement over a specified period of time. It assists in analyzing the volatility involved in price changes of any asset, then selecting the best time for trading and achieving trading consistency.

J. Welles Wilder introduced this method in his 1978 book "New Concepts in Technical Trading Systems" to evaluate commodity risk by calculating the volatility of the commodity. Although it is used to forecast trends, it does not show the direction of price movements.

The Average True Range indicator application predicts trend changes by using the average of True Ranges and showing volatility.

If ATR is increasing, it indicates greater volatility for swing or momentum trading. Similarly, if ATR is decreasing, it could suggest that the stock is experiencing lower volatility, which may provide opportunities for range-bound trading or mean reversion trading.

In essence, it adheres to the basic concept of a security's range (high price-low price); if the range is wide, volatility is wide, and vice versa.

The True Range (TR) at any given time period is the greatest of the following:

* The difference between the current high and current low

- The difference between the current high and previous close
- The difference between the current low and previous close

When the first ATR has been calculated, the following formula is used:

Current ATR =

where n = number of periods (typically 14 periods)

The ATR indicator is non-directional. It is more concerned with predicting the occurrence of a trend shift than with predicting its precise direction. It never defines the direction, such as whether or not a bullish sentiment will occur.

It is more useful as an indicator for identifying potential trend changes, setting stop-loss orders, and determining position size (stop losses and position size are addressed in the Risk Management chapter). For example, if the ATR is high, it suggests that the security is experiencing a high level of volatility, and traders may need to adjust their stop-loss orders to account for this volatility. Alternatively, if the ATR is low, it may suggest that the security is experiencing low volatility, and traders may need to adjust their position size to account for potential smaller price movements.

Also, the ATR is always used in association with other trading tools like support and resistance indicators and trendlines. Below is a chart with an ATR indicator showing a mid-range volatility of the traded security:

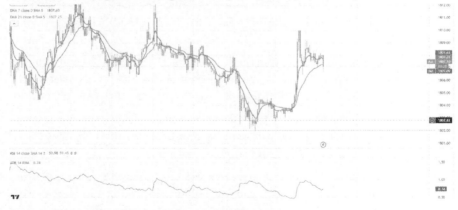

The ATR indicator is useful for securities that experience high levels of volatility or that exhibit strong trends, as these conditions can create potential trading opportunities

And that brings us to the end of this chapter. Meanwhile, in the next three chapters, you'll discover more about charts and patterns and what technical indicators work well with each, starting with why "the trend is your friend."

Key Takeaways

- Trend indicators are tools for identifying the direction of the price movement of a financial asset over a given period of time.

- The longer the moving average's period, the more reliable it is.

- The Fibonacci retracement tool is based on the belief that prices frequently retrace a predictable portion of a move, after which they continue in the original direction.

- Securities that have a tendency to experience momentum and trending behavior, as well as those that are not highly volatile or subject to sudden price spikes or drops, can work well with the RSI and Stochastic Oscillator indicators.

- When the Volume RSI crosses above the 50% level, it is considered a bullish signal, as the bullish volume is stronger than the bearish volume.

Chapter 4

Riding the Waves

"A good trend following system will keep you in the market until there is evidence that the trend has changed."
– Richard Dennis

Richard Dennis is a rich, well-known genius and pioneer of commodity trading. He is most popular for his "Turtle Traders" experiment, where he taught a group of novice traders his trading system based on technical analysis.

Dennis's story stands out among those of many veteran traders who have gone through the highs and lows of financial markets. His exceptional success can be attributed to his early start, sharp management skills, and clear trading strategies. More so, many traders who learned from him have achieved success in their own right today.

Dennis began his trading career at seventeen on the Chicago Mercantile Exchange trading floor. While he started off as an order runner, he reportedly borrowed $1,600 at age twenty-one, and turned it into $200 million within a decade by trading commodities. So, by age twenty-six, he had already become a millionaire trader.

In the inflationary markets of the 1970s, marked by repeated crop failures and the "Great Russian Grain Robbery" of 1972, Dennis made significant profits by buying new weekly and monthly highs in trending markets. However, he didn't succeed without facing significant volatility.

So what is Dennis's turtle experiment all about?

Well, it's all about following the trend—something I like to call "riding the wave."

Although this trading strategy will incur losses when the market ranges, it's guaranteed to earn you huge profits when the market makes big moves. So, you want to focus on only trading securities that always trend.

Trend following is an effective trading strategy to adopt. In fact, it has many followers and is almost like a religion for some investors and traders. This is why I want us to explore this concept in this chapter. Subsequently, we will dive deep into trend analysis and how to trade the trend profitably by identifying entry and exit points.

"The Trend Is Your Friend"

You might have heard the popular saying, "The trend is your friend." And indeed, it is. This expression comes from the common knowledge that it's easier and more profitable to trade in the direction of a trend than against it. The concept suggests that a security currently trading in a certain direction will continue to do so until it reaches a point where it breaks out and moves in the opposite direction.

In essence, trend following is all about following a market trend. Basically, you buy a security when the trend is up, then sell it once the trend is ending and try to break out to the downside. And as you do so, you must ensure to let your winners roll while cutting your losses. See? Easy-peasy!

Part of the meaning behind "the trend is your friend" is the basis for momentum trading, which we will cover in detail in Chapter 7.

Momentum trading involves identifying the trends and price movements of various assets with the assumption that if an asset is rising in value, it will likely continue to do so. Similarly, if an asset declines in value, it will continue in that direction. It is a common observation that investors and traders tend to act predictably. For instance, bulls will continue to follow the upward momentum and may eventually suffer a downfall. On the other hand, bears resist the trend and seek opportunities when the market is expected to turn downward.

So, once you've identified an established trend, you must trust and follow it.

But what if the trend reverses?

Also, how do we know it's happening, and how do we know whether a move down is a ruse or a genuine deal?

Well, that's where trend analysis comes into play. We need to be able to analyze a trend to give us some lead time and help us understand when a trend change is taking place. We don't want to be on top or the bottom. If that happens, it will be a fantastic moment.

Trying to predict the exact top or bottom of the market is a losing strategy, as it can lead to endless frustration and disappointment. Instead, our focus should be on identifying trends and adapting to changes in those trends.

Market price movements constantly fluctuate, and it is important to step back and observe the bigger picture to identify long-term trends. These trends can be either upward (an uptrend) or downward (a downtrend), and their duration can vary depending on their steepness. Generally, steeper trends tend to have shorter durations. Ultimately, our goal is to survive and thrive by navigating the market with the changing winds of trends.

We can use technical analysis to analyze a trend and make an educated guess about its future direction. But before we proceed, I must say this: this system of riding the wave works best for securities with strong fundamental metrics, like strong and improving cash flow and earnings.

Understanding Trend Analysis

Trend analysis is a technical analysis technique that traders and investors use to identify and analyze market trends over a specific period. Market trends show the general direction in which a particular asset or market moves over time and can be influenced by various factors, including economic indicators, market sentiment, and investor behavior.

Market trends can be either bullish or bearish, indicating a rising or falling market. And although a trend is not always a straight line, it can also include temporary reversals or fluctuations along the way. Nonetheless, understanding and analyzing market trends can help investors make insightful decisions about when to buy or sell an asset.

Another benefit of trend analysis is that it allows traders to identify the current market trend and predict its future direction. That way, we can tell when it's the right time to buy or sell a security.

Looking at market trends on the chart, you will quickly observe that they fall into three categories:

Upward Trends

An increase in the security price usually reflects a favorable situation and suggests that the security is a worthwhile investment. Uptrends are identified by a series of higher highs and higher lows, meaning that the asset's price generally increases over time. Upward trends are also indicative of a bull market, so as a trader, you should be looking to buy the security during this period.

Downward Trends

Downward trends imply a fall in the value of the traded securities. For example, a significant decline in a company's profits may cause traders and investors to be wary of a risky stock's declining price. This also applies to other economic and financial factors trending downhill. Unlike uptrends, downtrends are marked by a series of lower highs and lower lows, indicating that the asset's price generally decreases over time. A decrease in the price of company stock indicates the presence of a bearish market. In such scenarios, you only want to place a sell trade since the price may decline.

Sideways/Horizontal Trend

Sideways trends are characterized by a period when the market moves within a specific price range, indicating that the stock price is relatively stable or stagnant. These trends show that the stock is making neither significant gain nor loss but moving within a narrow price range. While a sideways trend may occasionally move up or down for a short period, making investment decisions based on this type of trend is generally considered risky.

Below, I have shared the different strategies we can use to analyze these different trend types:

Moving Averages (MAs)

You already know what MAs are, as we already covered them in Chapter 3. The main goal of using moving averages to study a trend is to reduce the influence of a security's short-term price volatility over a given period.

As a trader, you apply this strategy by entering long positions when a short-term MA (like a 50-Day MA) moves above a long-term MA (like a 200-Day MA). Conversely, you want to enter short positions when the short-term MA moves below the long-term MA.

Let's study the case of Alphabet Inc (Google) for example:

From the above image, you can see how the 200-Day MA (red line) crosses the 50-Day MA, sometime in April, giving a signal to enter a short position.

Momentum Indicators

This approach can be used to identify the strengths and weaknesses of a stock's pricing.

As we discussed in Chapter 3, momentum measures the rate at which a stock's price rises or falls. And I shared the two common examples of momentum indicators with you: the RSI and Stochastic Oscillator.

This approach takes a long or short position when the price of a security is moving up or down with so much momentum. However, you can use this method to close out your long position when the company's shares lose momentum. I usually recommend using the relative strength index (RSI) when executing this technique.

Here's a stock price chart of Alphabet Inc (Google):

You can see that the company's shares trended higher as RSI momentum increased and remained above the middle band of the oscillator. Thus, this clearly indicates a buy signal.

Trendlines

A trendline is a series of lines and curves used in technical analysis to discover price patterns. They are known as "diagonal support and resistance lines" because traders use them to identify support and resistance on a stock price chart across diagonal levels.

When the equity shares of any company are trending higher, traders who use this trend analysis approach enter long positions. Furthermore, this strategy places a stop-loss order below the resistance or support levels, i.e., the major trendline.

Let's look at the example of Alphabet Inc (Google) once again.

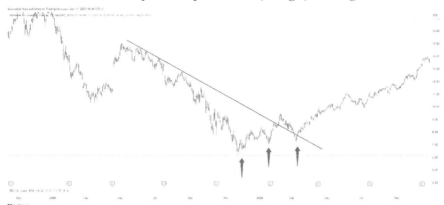

We can see how the stock of this internet technology begins to trend higher from the bottom of the market, creating higher highs and higher lows until it crosses the sketched trendline and breaks out in the opposite direction. As a result, the downward trend has finished, and the market is set to begin going upward.

The approach of waiting for a trend to break out of the drawn trendline before entering it is known as the "breakout" strategy. It helps us determine when the price of an asset breaks through a key level of diagonal resistance or support, often with high trading volume, indicating a potential shift in the overall trend.

As you can note from the chart above, a breakout above the resistance signals a bullish trend. Likewise, a breakout below support could signal a bearish trend. Typically, breakout signals are an opportunity for us to either enter or exit positions. For more clarification, we will go into more detail about trading trendlines in the next section of this chapter, so hang on.

Analyzing market trends has several key advantages as an investment analysis technique. It is a simple method that allows for easy comparison of the performance of multiple companies over the same period. Comparing trends can help you determine which companies are stronger or weaker in a given sector.

Trend analysis is also useful for examining the entire financial market to identify potential changes in the trend, either positive or negative.

As a trader, it is essential to identify safe and logical options and strategies and use technical indicators, such as MAs and RSI, to confirm trading decisions. In the long run, this will help you increase profits and minimize losses.

Trading Trendlines

Now that you have a broad idea of what trendlines are, it's time to advance our lessons. The chart below shows that a trendline is a straight line connecting two or more price points on a chart.

As indicated in the chart above, trendlines are drawn on price charts, preferably candlestick charts. In an uptrend, the trendline is drawn by connecting the higher lows, while in a downtrend, the trendline is drawn by connecting the lower highs. Trendlines can be subjective depending on where you begin and end the plots and the chart time range employed.

We use trendlines to identify the direction and strength of a trend in the price of a security over a period of time. But unlike moving averages, trendlines don't consider any averages, as it's purely a visual tool.

Besides showing a trend's direction, trendlines also help us pinpoint potential areas of support and resistance. An upward trendline is drawn by connecting two or more low points on the chart, while a downward trendline is drawn by connecting two or more high points. These lines help traders to identify key levels where the price may reverse direction or find support/resistance, which can help them make better trading decisions.

For instance, if the price of a security approaches an uptrend line, that might be a good time to buy the security, as the chances the trend will continue rising are high. On the other hand, if the price of a security approaches a downtrend line, that might be a good time to sell the security, as there is a high probability that the trend will continue downward.

The significance of a trendline depends on the number of touchpoints. For instance, the char*t above shows a trendline with three touchpoints. And the more touchpoints a trendline has, the more important it is because it indicates that other traders are also paying attention to those levels.*

However, the strength of the trend is determined by whether the touchpoints hold or not. If a trendline is strong, it will resist any attempts to break the touchpoints and continue to follow the trend. This reinforces the trend, making it stronger. However, if the trendline breaks, prices can reverse suddenly.

*Below, I hav*e put together different unique ways trendlines can be used efficiently:

Use Trendlines That are Applicable to Your Trading Time Frame

The trendlines on a chart can vary depending on the time frame used. For instance, the security's trend may differ on different trendlines by showing an uptrend in a four-hour time frame and a downtrend in a fifteen-minute time frame. Therefore, it is important to determine which time frames are most relevant for your trades when using trendlines. We'll talk more about time frames in the next section, so there's no need to worry if you already find the subject confusing.

Use Trendlines for Support/Resistance

As I've already explained, a trendline can be used as a support level in an uptrend. To enter an uptrend, traders should watch for pullbacks and ensure that the trendline is rising, deflecting any tests on pullbacks to bounce higher. During the pullback, traders can enter a long position either by testing the trendline or bouncing off it. Conversely, traders looking to short for downtrends can wait for reversions to the falling trendline before entering short positions. If the trendline breaks, it can be used as a stop-loss area. In that sense, trendlines are useful for identifying good entry and exit levels.

Use Trendlines to Identify Trend Reversals

Earlier, I talked about the breakout strategy using the trendline. If a security price falls below an uptrend line and cannot bounce back up from it, the up-trend may break down. Conversely, a breakout occurs when the price crosses a descending trendline and maintains pullbacks above it, reversing the trend. This can be a reliable entry or exit point for traders looking to capitalize on such situations or maintain stops at those levels.

Additionally, two trendlines can be used to trade within channels, with one being drawn between the price highs and the other between the lows. The Gold chart below is a perfect example of this method:

Trades can be made by buying at the lower trendline when the price bounces off it and then selling or shorting at the upper trendline when the price reverses. This strategy involves trading within the channel created by the upper and lower trendlines.

The greater the trend channel, the larger the time frame. So, the idea here is to allocate the appropriate number of shares and manage the fluctuations.

However, avoid one of the most typical mistakes when trading with trendlines: entering and departing too quickly. It is common for traders to set a stop-loss order when the price tests or overshoots the trendline. However, they may later regret their decision to exit the trade because the trendline ultimately holds, and the price reverses back in the direction of the trend. So, leaving too soon makes you miss out on potential profits.

Nonetheless, giving yourself some breathing room is a good idea so you don't get too hung up on the trend too soon. The longer time frames necessitate a larger gap. Likewise, you should also wait for a reversal to enter or scale into a position at several moments, such as the trendline test, overshoot, and reversal, for entrances. You can also include a momentum indicator, such as a stochastic or RSI, to provide an overbought or oversold gauge to help you pace your entries and exits about the trendline.

Time Frames

Traders of all monetary sizes and temperaments trade the financial market. Indeed, both short-term scalpers and long-term traders are looking at the same securities simultaneously, trying to decide how to place or alter their transactions.

However, even if they look at the same asset, they do not look at the same chart time ranges. Short-term traders, for example, are more likely to look at currency charts that range from one minute to thirty minutes, but long-term traders are more likely to look at daily, weekly, and monthly charts.

Trends, support, resistance lines, and technical indicators seem very different on a one-minute chart than a daily one. For example, look at the daily chart of US Oil below, and you'll see that it appears to be in a downtrend structure:

Now, let's look at the one-hour chart time frame:

Obviously, you can see that US Oil is now showing an uptrend structure. So the question is, which chart is right?

Is US Oil in an uptrend or a downtrend?

Well, here comes the real deal: successful traders using technical analysis trade with a bias toward the long-term trend. It has had a long time to establish itself, and it will take a large surge of momentum to change its direction.

Therefore, you should always be aware of trends, and support and resistance levels across multiple time frames. This will help you identify how strong various trends and levels of support and resistance are. Ultimately, using multiple time frames on your charts enables you to expand your technical analysis.

However, I recommend that you analyze securities with at least three different time frames, starting from a higher time frame to a lower time frame, before deciding whether to go long or short. Usually, I would name these time frames as shown below:

- **Market trend chart:** This is the longer-term chart, usually the monthly, weekly, or daily time frame. As the name suggests, the market trend chart helps you identify the predominant trend you should be looking to trade with. If the security in the trend chart is trending upward, you should be looking to place buy orders. But if the trend chart is trending downward, you should be looking to sell the security.

- **Behavior/signal chart:** This is the time frame you use or trade in, usually the four-hour or one-hour time frame. The signal chart is your most important chart. It provides the trading signals that tell you when to look for buying and selling opportunities based on your trading strategy.

- **Entry/timing chart:** This is the shorter-term chart where you usually decide to enter a trade. The timing chart helps you know when to enter and exit a trade. Every point counts when you are a trader, so the more accurately you can identify your entry and exit points, the more money you can keep in your account. For this chart, you want to be looking at the thirty-minute, fifteen-minute, or five-minute time frame.

Now, which time frames you should use or combine depends on your trading style and investment goals, and the security being traded.

Day traders, for instance, are always looking for quick profits from intra-day price movements. And so, the recommended time frames to use are Daily for market trends, one-hour to study market behavior, and fifteen-minute or five-minute for placing trades.

Meanwhile, swing traders usually use the Weekly for market trends, Daily to study market behavior, and one-hour or fifteen-minute for placing trades.

Other traders and investors may use longer-term time frames, such as daily, weekly, or monthly charts, to identify longer-term trends in the market.

In the end, the multi-time-frame analysis is a collection of various factors that combine to generate an opinion. It offers traders a broader perspective from a longer time frame. A trade setup can be detected at a lower time frame, and entry-exit can be prepared at an even lower time frame. This allows us to plan ahead of time what and how we will trade. Better risk management is also possible because stop losses can be fine-tuned in a shorter time frame.

However, before you start riding the waves and applying the multi-time-frame analysis, it is important to get familiarized with price action, support and resistance levels, trendlines, technical indicators, candlestick patterns, and chart patterns.

Fortunately, we've covered these subjects, except for candlestick patterns and chart patterns, which we will discuss explicitly in Chapters 5 and 6, respectively.

Key Takeaways

- "The Trend is Your Friend" is a concept that suggests that a security currently trading in a particular direction will continue to do so until it reaches a point where it breaks out and moves in the opposite direction.

- Trend analysis is a technical analysis technique that traders and investors use to identify and analyze a market trend over a specific period.

- The three strategies for analyzing different trend types are through the use of moving averages, momentum indicators, and trendlines.

- Securities usually have different trend structures across multiple time frames. Hence, it's important to consider multiple time frames when analyzing trends.

Chapter 5
Lighting the Way

"I believe my most important skill is an ability to perceive patterns in the market. I think this aptitude for pattern recognition is probably related to my heavy involvement with music."
— Linda Bradford Raschke

Linda Bradford Raschke's quote above is a testament that patterns are everything in the market. And I'm not talking about decorated, ornamented patterns here. No, I'm referring to candlestick patterns, which form the basis of every strategy used in trading the financial market.

Candlestick patterns are among the most important tools for traders to analyze the financial market. Their use is based on the concept that candlestick patterns can identify market psychology and human behavior on a chart. So, by recognizing these patterns, traders can predict future price movements and make better trading decisions.

Fortunately, Raschke happens to be one trader who has become widely known for her use of candlestick patterns over the past three decades. She began her career as a market maker in equity options and was a member of and floor trader on two exchanges.

In the early 1990s, Raschke founded LBRGroup, Inc., a professional money management organization, after becoming a registered commodity trading advisor (CTA). Since then, she has been a principal trader for various hedge funds and has led commercial hedging programs in addition to conducting successful CTA programs.

Raschke's success as a trader has been largely due to her ability to use technical analysis to identify market trends and recognize and interpret candlestick patterns. She has used these patterns to make big wins in the market, and her strategies have been praised for their effectiveness. Raschke's approach to trading is based on a combination of technical analysis and market psychology, and she is known for her ability to adapt her strategies to changing market conditions.

Just like Raschke, we, too, need to learn to study candlestick patterns and interpret them. That way, we can gain a deeper understanding of market psychology and make better trading decisions, such as knowing when to enter and exit the market.

A Bright Idea From the Rice Fields of Japan

Candlestick charting is a popular technical tool traders use to analyze financial markets. It was developed in Japan by Munehisa Homma in the 18th century to track the price fluctuations of rice, the country's primary commodity.

Homma, often called the father of Japanese candlesticks, was born in 1724 in Sakata, an important port and hub for rice trading. At the time, the Homma family owned large rice plantations and was largely involved in rice trading.

After the passing of his father in 1750, Homma, the youngest son, took on the responsibility of managing the family's capital, which was unusual since it was customary for the eldest son to take over the father's business. Nonetheless, this demonstrates his outstanding commercial acumen. Around the same time, a rice exchange was established in Sakata. Homma began trading on it, eventually expanding his activities to Osaka and Edo, where he made a substantial fortune.

Rumors have it that Homma became so adept at trading that he executed 100 profitable transactions. Some sources suggest that he earned the modern-day equivalent of $10 billion trading in the Japanese rice markets. While this may seem far-fetched, it is worth remembering that Homma is credited with creating a system that is still widely used today.

When the Japanese government officially authorized the exchange trade in rice, Homma was invited to serve as a financial advisor and bestowed the title of a samurai.

Western traders refined Homma's approach in the early 20th century, with Steve Nison being the first to introduce candlestick charts to the western hemisphere with his book *Japanese Candlestick Charting Techniques*, which was first published in 1991. Today, traders worldwide widely use candlesticks to analyze stocks, futures, currencies, and other financial instruments.

The original Japanese candlestick chart was a simple chart of the price of rice over time. Rice was the most important commodity in Japan, and its price fluctuated because of weather conditions, political events, and supply and demand. So rice traders adopted the charting style, using candlestick shapes to represent price movements visually.

Each candlestick depicts a specific time period and is composed of a rectangle, called the body, and two lines, called the wicks or shadows. The shape of the candlestick was determined by the opening and closing prices of rice during that period and the high and low prices (more on the candlestick anatomy later).

Candlesticks are useful in trading analysis because they provide a visual picture of what is happening in the market. In fact, we can gain useful information about the open, high, low, and close prices simply by looking at a candlestick, which will give us an idea about the price movement.

Candlesticks are flexible; they can be employed alone or with technical indicators, as we discussed in Chapter 3. I, for one, use candlesticks around support and resistance levels, trendlines, and other technical tools, which you will learn about in subsequent chapters.

By analyzing the patterns of candlesticks near support and resistance levels, we can gain insight into the behavior of buyers and sellers and anticipate potential price movements.

The Anatomy of a Candlestick

Japanese candlesticks are made using the opening, highest, lowest, and closing prices of the chosen time frame.

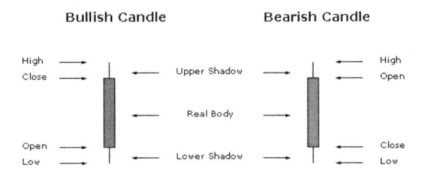

As you can see in the figure above, the top of the body depicts the opening price, while the bottom represents the closing price.

The shadows, also known as wicks, represent that period's high and low prices. The upper wick extends from the top of the body to the highest price reached during the period, while the lower wick extends from the bottom to the lowest price reached during the period.

The length of the wicks indicates the degree of price fluctuation during the period.

The color of the body can vary, but, typically, green or white represents a bullish market, while red or black represents a bearish market.

In essence, we can say that a candlestick is bullish if the close is above the open. When that happens, the market is rising in this period, and bullish candlesticks will be displayed as green or white.

However, if the close is below the open, we can infer that the candlestick is bearish, which shows that the market is falling in this session. And such a bearish candle will be displayed as red or black.

Notwithstanding, it makes no difference what color you select because you can use whatever color you desire based on the trading software you use. The most crucial thing is to understand the nuances of open and close prices.

Candlestick Body Size

A candlestick's body represents the difference between a security's opening and closing prices throughout the specified period. As a result, a candle's open and close prices cause its body size to change. And we can use this data to estimate the volume of securities traded during that period.

Long vs. Short

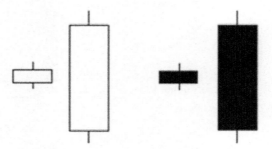

Long bodies signify major buying or selling pressure; if a candlestick's close is above the open with a long body, buyers are stronger and taking control of the market during this time frame.

In contrast, a bearish candlestick with an open above the close and a long body indicates that selling pressure is in charge of the market throughout the selected time frame.

Likewise, short and small bodies imply that there has been little buying or selling activity.

Candlestick Shadows/Wicks

The upper and lower shadows tell us a lot about the trading session. The upper shadows represent the session's high, while the lower shadows represent the session's low. Candlesticks with extended shadows indicate that trade occurred far after the opening and closing.

Long Shadows

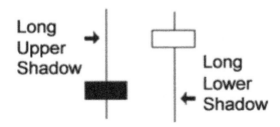

Japanese candlesticks with short shadows suggest that most trade activities occurred near the opening and closing. For example, if a candlestick has a long upper shadow and a shorter lower shadow, it shows that buyers exercised their muscles and raised the bid price. But, for some reason, sellers stepped in and drove the price back down, bringing the session to a close near the open price.

A Japanese candlestick with a lengthy bottom shadow and a short higher wick indicates that sellers pressured the price. But, for some reason, buyers poured in and drove prices back up, bringing the session close to its open price.

Generally, candlestick charts are important because they provide visual cues to help traders identify trends, reversals, and other patterns in the market. For example, a long green daily candlestick with little or no wick on the bottom indicates that buyers have dominated the market throughout the day, pushing the price up. This may suggest that the bullish trend will continue in the near future. Conversely, a long red daily candlestick with little or no wick on the top indicates that sellers have dominated the market, pushing the price down. This may suggest that the bearish trend will continue shortly.

In addition to identifying support and resistance levels, candlestick charts can help traders identify potential price reversals. For example, a long bullish trend followed by a long bearish candlestick may indicate that the market is about to reverse its direction, suggesting that sellers have taken control of the market. Similarly, a long bearish trend followed by a bullish candlestick may indicate that the market is about to reverse its direction, suggesting that buyers have taken control of the market.

But not to worry; we will learn about all of these patterns and actions in the next section.

Candlestick Patterns

Usually, we don't use just one candlestick to analyze the financial market. Instead, we use multiple candlesticks, like two or three candlesticks, which makes a candlestick pattern.

As traders, we aim to recognize these candlestick patterns around major support and resistance levels. Doing so will enable us to determine when to enter and exit a trade.

Numerous candlestick patterns signify a market opportunity—some provide insight into strong buying pressures, while others offer insight into strong selling pressures. In contrast, others enable us to see areas of indecision or continuations in the market.

So before you begin trading, you must understand the fundamentals of candlestick patterns and how they might influence your selections.

Bullish Candlestick Patterns

Bullish candlestick patterns are chart patterns that suggest that the price of an asset is likely to rise. One or more candlesticks form these patterns and can be used by traders to make buy or long positions. Below are the most common bullish candlestick patterns you should focus on:

1. **Hammer**

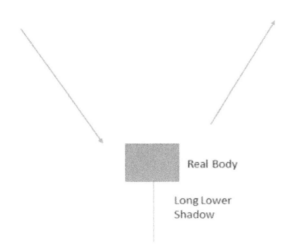

This candlestick pattern emerges at the end of a downtrend, characterized by a compact body indicating a narrow price range between opening and closing prices, a prolonged wick below the body, and little to no wick above.

This pattern suggests buyers have started participating in the market, leading to an upward price movement. The extended wick below the body confirms that the bears' attempt to push prices down has failed, while the bulls' attempt to take control is evident from the swift upward movement before the period closed.

2. **Inverse hammer**

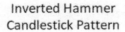

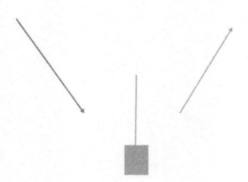

This candlestick pattern emerges at the end of a downtrend, characterized by a compact body indicating a narrow price range between opening and closing prices, a long wick above the body, and little to no wick below.

This pattern suggests buyers have started participating in the market, leading to an upward price movement. The extended wick below the body confirms that the bears' attempt to push prices down has failed, while the bulls' attempt to take control is evident from the swift upward movement before the period closed.

3. Bullish engulfing

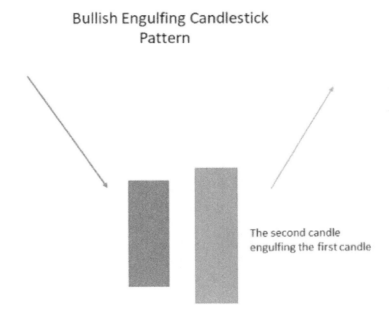

Bullish Engulfing Candlestick
Pattern

The second candle
engulfing the first candle

This pattern is made up of two candlesticks: the first is bearish, while the other is bullish. In this case, the bullish candlestick completely engulfs the real body of the previous bearish candlestick.

This confirms an increase in bearish and bullish activities—that bearish momentum is losing steam, and the bulls are taking control, potentially leading to a shift of overall market sentiment towards bullishness.

4. Piercing line

Piercing Pattern Candlestick Pattern

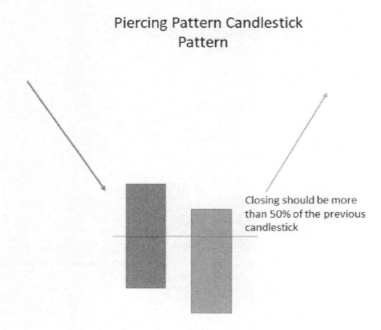

Closing should be more than 50% of the previous candlestick

When there is a downtrend, a bullish signal may appear, which involves a long bearish candle followed by a bullish candle that opens at a new low and closes at least halfway up the body of the previous candle. This two-bar indicator is considered reliable in signaling a trend reversal, with the strength of the reversal being proportional to the height of the second bullish candle.

The piercing line pattern suggests that the bulls are starting to take control, and a trend reversal may be imminent.

5. Morning star

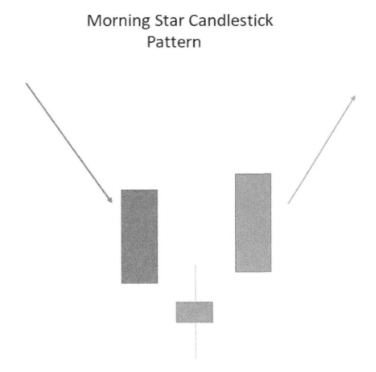

Morning Star Candlestick
Pattern

This pattern has three candlesticks. The first candlestick is a bearish candle. The second type of candle is the "star," which is a small-bodied candle that opens at the closure of the previous candle or a gap below it, signaling that a trend is shifting from bearish to bullish. The third is a bullish candle that gaps up and closes above the midpoint of the first candlestick. It indicates a potential trend reversal.

6.   Three white soldiers

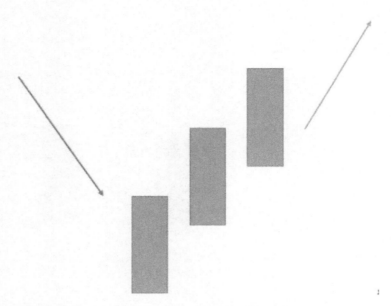

Three white soldiers is a candlestick pattern comprising three consecutive long bullish candlesticks with higher closing prices, indicating a strong uptrend. It suggests buyers are firmly in control of the market, and a trend reversal may be imminent.

7. Bullish harami

Bullish Harami
Candlestick Pattern

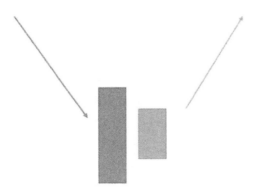

This pattern has two candlesticks, where the first candlestick is bearish, while the second candlestick is bullish with a small real body completely engulfed by the previous bearish candlestick.

A bullish harami indicates that the bearish momentum is slowing down, and the bulls are starting to gain control, potentially leading to a trend reversal.

8. Bullish harami cross

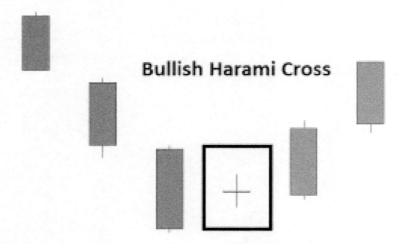

Bullish Harami Cross

This pattern resembles a bullish harami, but the second candlestick has a doji instead of a small real body. Like a bullish harami, this pattern also suggests that the bearish momentum is slowing down, and the bulls are starting to gain control, potentially leading to a trend reversal.

Bearish Candlestick Patterns

Bearish candlestick patterns are chart patterns that signal a potential trend reversal to the downside. They are formed when the opening price is higher than the closing price, indicating that sellers have taken control of the market. Here are the most common bearish candlestick patterns:

1. Hanging man

Hanging Man Candlestick Pattern

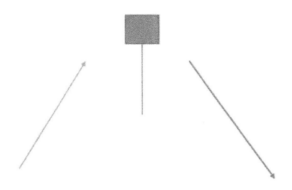

The hanging man candlestick pattern emerges at the apex of an uptrend and is a bearish reversal pattern. It features a short lower shadow and a small genuine body, indicating that buyers have lost control, and sellers are entering the market. The long lower shadow suggests that buyers are still present but cannot push the price up. The hanging man pattern could indicate a potential trend reversal if it forms after a long uptrend.

2. Shooting star

Shooting Star
Candlestick Pattern

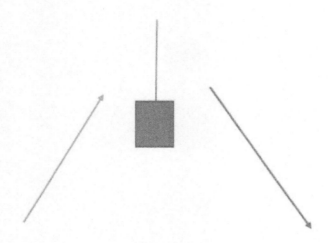

The shooting star candlestick pattern is made up of a bearish signal that appears during an uptrend. It has a small body with a long wick above it and little to no wick below. The long wick indicates that there is resistance to further upward movement and suggests that a bearish reversal may be imminent.

The shooting star indicates that sellers have entered the market and are pushing the price down. Likewise, the long upper shadow suggests that buyers are still present but cannot push the price up. This pattern could indicate a potential trend reversal if it forms after a long uptrend.

3. Bearish engulfing

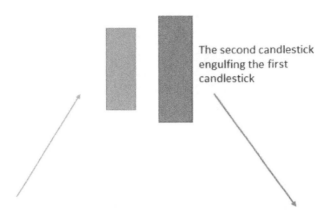

**Bearish Engulfing
Candlestick Pattern**

The second candlestick engulfing the first candlestick

This is the inverse of a bullish engulfing pattern, in which the body of a subsequent bullish candle engulfs the body of a preceding bullish candle. This pattern forms after an uptrend. It consists of two candlesticks, where the first candlestick is bullish and the second is bearish, with the bearish candlestick completely engulfing the real body of the previous bullish candlestick.

This pattern indicates that the bullish momentum is losing steam, and the bears are taking control, potentially leading to a trend reversal.

4. Evening star

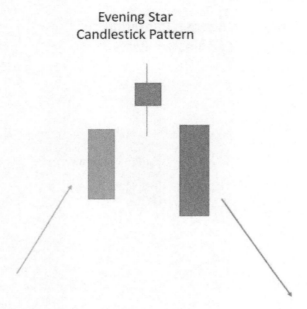

Evening Star
Candlestick Pattern

The "evening star" is the second candle with a small body in a three-bar pattern that can indicate a shift from a bullish to a bearish trend. Usually, the opening price of the middle candle is at or above the closing price of the preceding candle. Sometimes, you may also see a gap between the previous candle's body and the next candle's opening.

The evening star pattern represents a possible top and, thus, a possible signal to sell.

5. Three black crows

Three Black Crows
Candlestick Pattern

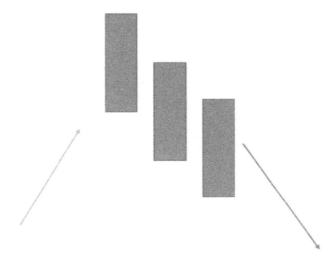

This three-candle pattern is the inverse of the three white soldiers pattern, indicating a shift away from bullish control at the peak of an uptrend. It comprises three consecutive bearish bars that open within the body of the previous bar and close below its closing.

This pattern indicates that sellers are firmly in control of the market, and a trend reversal may be imminent.

6. Dark cloud cover

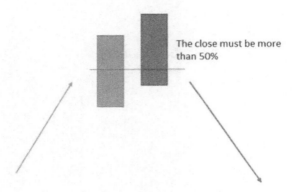

This two-candle bearish reversal pattern occurs at the top of a bullish trend and is the bearish inverse of the piercing line. The first bullish candle is followed by a bearish candle that opens at a new high and ends at least halfway down the preceding bar's body. The reversal signal's strength is proportional to the length of the second candle.

The piercing line pattern is obviously conceptually and mathematically related to this design. It indicates that buyers have failed to maintain control, and the bears are taking over, potentially leading to a trend reversal.

7. Bearish harami

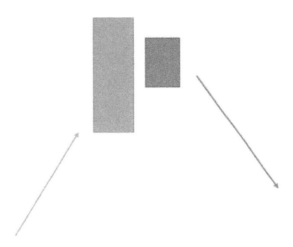

Bearish Harami
Candlestick Pattern

The bearish harami candlestick pattern is a bearish reversal pattern that consists of two candlesticks. The first candlestick is bullish, while the next is bearish, with a small real body completely engulfed by the previous day's bullish candlestick. This pattern indicates that the bullish momentum is slowing down, and the bears are starting to gain control, potentially leading to a trend reversal.

8. Bearish harami cross

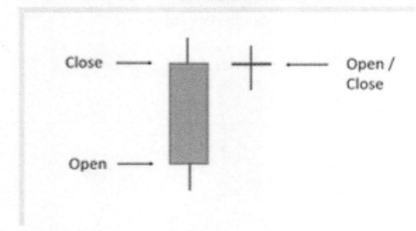

The bearish harami cross is similar to the bearish harami candlestick pattern, but the second candlestick has a doji instead of a small real body. This pattern also indicates that the bullish momentum is slowing down, and the bears are starting to gain control, potentially leading to a trend reversal.

Continuation or Neutral Candlestick Patterns

Continuation or neutral candlestick patterns are chart patterns that indicate a temporary pause in the prevailing trend or suggest that the trend is likely to continue. Here are examples of continuation or neutral candlestick patterns:

1. Doji

The doji is a neutral pattern that forms when the opening and closing prices are the same or very close to each other. It can signal indecision or a potential reversal.

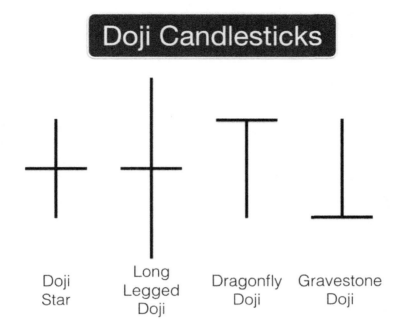

Doji Candlesticks

Doji Star

Long Legged Doji

Dragonfly Doji

Gravestone Doji

The following are the four different types of dojis:

- **Four-price doji:** Also known as a doji star, a four-price doji is a doji with equal opening and closing prices that also match the highest and lowest prices of the trading session. This pattern indicates significant indecision in the market and can signal a potential reversal.

- **Long-legged doji:** A long-legged doji is a doji with very long upper and lower wicks, indicating that the price moved up and down significantly during the trading session but ultimately closed at the same level. This pattern suggests the market is highly uncertain and can signal a potential reversal.

- **Dragonfly doji:** A dragonfly doji is a doji that has a long lower wick and no upper wick, indicating that the price opened and closed at the highest level of the trading session. This pattern can suggest a bullish reversal or a potential support level.

- **Gravestone doji:** A gravestone doji is a doji that has a long upper wick and no lower wick, indicating that the price opened and closed at the lowest level of the trading session. This pattern can suggest a bearish reversal or a potential resistance level.

2. Spinning top

Spinning Top
Candlestick Pattern

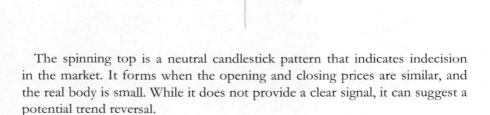

The spinning top is a neutral candlestick pattern that indicates indecision in the market. It forms when the opening and closing prices are similar, and the real body is small. While it does not provide a clear signal, it can suggest a potential trend reversal.

3. Falling three methods

Falling Three Methods
Candlestick Pattern

The falling three methods is a bearish continuation pattern that consists of a long bearish candlestick followed by three consecutive small-bodied bullish candlesticks and another long bearish candlestick. This pattern indicates that the bearish trend is likely to continue.

4. Rising three methods

Rising Three Methods
Candlestick Pattern

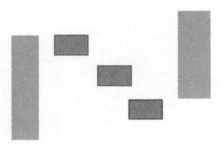

The rising three methods is a bullish continuation pattern that consists of a long bullish candlestick followed by three consecutive small-bodied bearish candlesticks and another long bullish candlestick. This pattern implies that the bullish trend is likely to continue.

As you can see, candlestick patterns provide valuable insight into market trends, and we use them to make informed investment decisions. So, understanding these patterns and combining them with other technical analysis tools is crucial to identifying profitable trading opportunities.

Fortunately, you'll discover and explore the fascinating world of chart patterns in the next chapter.

Key Takeaways

- Candlestick charting is a popular technical tool traders use to analyze financial markets.

- Japanese candlesticks are formed using the opening price, highest price, lowest price, and closing price of the chosen time frame.

- A candlestick's body represents the difference between a security's opening and closing prices throughout the specified period.

- The upper and lower shadows of a candlestick tell us a lot about a trading session.

- We use multiple candlesticks, like two or three candlesticks, which makes a candlestick pattern to analyze the market.

"Charts really are the 'footprint of money'."
— Fred McAllen

Mat is struggling to keep his small commerce business afloat as his competitor is beating him in sales. Eventually, he decides to go public and buys his competitor's business to expand and beat his competition, adding more stores to his business. This move allows him to negotiate lower prices for the household supplies he sells, helping his customers save more and using the profits to build more stores.

Lily, a trader and investor, learns of Mat's plans to expand his operation statewide and conducts her research on his business. She visits several of Mat's business stores and finds them bustling with customers. Then, after reviewing the business's financials, she concludes that it's a sound investment.

Lily then orders her trading partners to buy the stock at no higher than 16, causing panic in the stock market due to the weak economy and impending recession. The stock drops to 13, and Lily's team buys as much as possible without raising suspicion. The stock eventually rises to 19, but the economy remains bleak, so it falls to 12 shortly. Even so, Lily buys more, and the stock rises to 17.5 after Mat's business releases better-than-expected sales numbers.

As the years go by, the stock splits several times, and the business booms, with the stock hitting 29. But during the holiday season, Lily discovers a massive distribution problem, and the business overextends itself, unable to support adding one new store each week. As a result, Lily realizes it's time to sell and decides to dump the stock for no less than 32.15.

Unfortunately, news of poor holiday sales and distribution problems causes the stock to plummet 27% overnight, and analysts advise their clients to sell. However, despite analysts' recommendations, some investors buy the stock, leading to a brief price rise before another round of selling takes hold.

Over the next forty days, the stock drops by 24%, and Mat's company announces that earnings will come in well below consensus estimates due to the distribution problem. As a result, the business decides to stop expanding and concentrate on profitability.

Two years later, Mat announces that a new commerce model is available via the internet, called e-commerce, particularly dropshipping. He believes it's an opportunity to sell his household supplies online and reach a wider audience without relying only on his brick-and-mortar stores. Soon enough, Lily hears the announcement, is impressed, and starts buying the stock again.

If you visualize the price action of Mat's commerce business, you may recognize three patterns:

- When the company's stock reached two bottom price levels, 13 and 12.

- When the stock skyrocketed to the top, reaching two different price levels, 29 and 32.15.

- When the stock price first fell by 27% before a brief rise and then fell further by another 24%.

If we observe these three patterns that Mat's company stock made on the candlestick chart, we'll see they are what technical analysts refer to as a double bottom, a double top, and a flag chart pattern, respectively.

While some investors may view chart patterns as squiggles on a price chart, knowledgeable investors see them as the footprints of smart money. These footprints can indicate the actions of institutional investors, hedge funds, and other market professionals who have access to valuable information before it is available to the public. By analyzing these footprints, investors can gain insight into the market's direction and exploit profitable opportunities.

Legendary traders like Jesse Livermore, a day-trading pioneer, applied these concepts in their trading strategy and made a fortune. Jesse Livermore was a master of reading chart patterns and using them to his advantage in the stock market. One day, as he sat in his office, he noticed a familiar pattern forming on a chart of a certain stock. He had seen this pattern and knew it often signaled a trend reversal.

Livermore quickly bought many shares of the stock and waited for the trend to reverse. As predicted, the trend reversed, and the stock price rose rapidly. Livermore's quick thinking and keen eye for chart patterns had paid off once again, and he could sell his shares for a substantial profit.

Using chart analysis and other technical tools, Livermore was able to predict market trends. He knew that by carefully studying the charts and identifying trends, he could make well-informed trades that would lead to big profits.

Therefore, it pays to deeply understand the market if you must use technical analysis in your trading decisions—which is why you should look for chart patterns. In addition to candlestick patterns, chart patterns will help you identify trading opportunities quickly and decide whether to buy or sell a stock.

What Are Chart Patterns?

A chart pattern is a shape that appears on a price chart, which predicts the direction prices might go in next by using a series of trendlines or curves. It is a natural phenomenon characterized by swings in the price of a financial asset, and it's driven by various causes, including human activity.

Chart patterns are part of the bedrock of technical analysis, and the patterns you'll find in this chapter will tell you different things about various markets and securities. In technical analysis, we use chart patterns to find trends in an asset's price movement since the price usually makes an uptrend or downtrend structure.

Thus, as a trader, you need to familiarize yourself with these chart patterns to know what exact decision to take when you look at your chart. Any trader who has the knowledge and skill to recognize patterns and apply them to their decision-making process can increase their chances of correctly predicting where the price will move next. However, the skill required to interpret chart patterns correctly takes practice and commitment to build.

Since no scientific theory or physical law constrains chart patterns, their success depends on the number of market participants who pay attention to them. So, naturally, this means you want to focus on trading securities with more trading volume.

While many chart patterns are used in technical analysis, they all fall majorly into two categories: reversal and continuation patterns.

The major reversal chart patterns we'll cover in this chapter include double tops and bottoms, head and shoulders, and wedges, while the continuation patterns include flags, the cup with handle, rectangles, and triangles.

Generally, the longer a continuation and reversal pattern forms, the higher the price movement within it, and the more dramatic the expected move will be once the price breaks out.

There is no way of knowing if a pricing pattern will continue or reverse while it develops. As a result, traders must pay particular attention to trendlines (which are used to build the price pattern) and the direction in which the price eventually breaks. Traders should, however, presume that a price trend will continue in its current direction unless it is confirmed that it has reversed.

Also, while I have categorized the chart patterns in this chapter as continuation or reversal, several patterns, such as the rectangle and triangle patterns, can imply continuation or reversal depending on the conditions.

Double Top and Bottom

Double top and double bottom are chart patterns usually used in technical analysis to identify potential reversals in price trends.

Double Top

The double top chart pattern is a bearish reversal pattern that appears on price charts. It has an M shape, with two peaks of similar heights separated by a trough or a valley. The pattern occurs in an uptrend, where the price rises to a peak, then retraces, and rises again to form a second peak at around the same level as the first before retracing.

Neckline

The peaks of the double top chart pattern are considered resistance levels, while the trough is regarded as a support level. When the price approaches the second peak, it may face resistance at the same level as the first peak, as traders who missed out on the first opportunity may seek to sell at this level. Where the price does not break through the resistance level, it may signal that the upward trend has been exhausted, and the price may decline.

The double top pattern is confirmed when the price breaks below the support level, which indicates that the upward trend has likely ended and that a downward trend may follow. Traders may use the double top chart pattern to identify potential short-selling opportunities or exit long positions.

Double Bottom

The double bottom chart pattern is a technical analysis pattern used to identify a potential trend reversal in the market. The pattern has a "W" shape and signals a bullish reversal, indicating a downtrend's end and an uptrend's start.

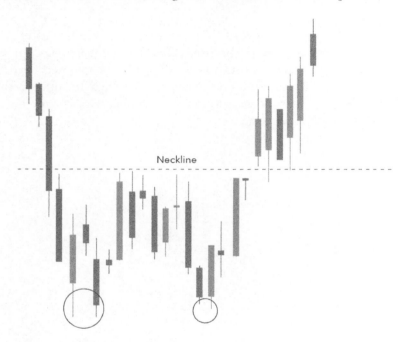

The double bottom pattern is formed when the price of an asset drops to a certain level, then bounces back up, but then falls again to the same level before bouncing back up again. This creates two lows around the same price level, forming the "W" shape.

The two lows are considered support levels, while the area between them is the resistance level. The double bottom pattern is established when the price breaks above the resistance level, indicating that the downtrend has ended and a new uptrend has started.

Meanwhile, I recommend you use trend, momentum, and volume indicators to help you predict double top and bottom chart patterns more accurately. Trend indicators, such as MAs, can help you to determine the direction of the trend and potential trend reversals. Likewise, momentum indicators, such as the RSI, can help you identify overbought conditions and divergence between price and momentum. And volume indicators, such as the OBV, can help you determine whether buying or selling pressure is increasing or decreasing. So, for example, a bullish crossover when the short-term MA crosses above the long-term MA can signal a trend reversal to the upside for a double bottom chart pattern. Also, an increasing trading volume when the price of a double bottom reaches the second low and then breaks above the resistance level indicates a stronger bullish trend.

Head and Shoulders (H&S)

The head and shoulders pattern is a technical analysis pattern used to identify potential reversals in the price trend of an asset. It is a reversal pattern that is made up of three peaks, and has the middle peak (the head/bottom) being higher than the other two (the shoulders).

The first peak, or left shoulder, is formed when the price rises to a high point, followed by a slight decline in price. The second peak, which could be the head or bottom, is formed when the price increases to a higher or lower point than the left shoulder, respectively, followed by a significant decline in price. Finally, the third peak, or right shoulder, is formed when the price rises again, but only to a level below the head, followed by another decline in price.

The head and shoulders pattern is complete the moment the price breaks through the neckline, which is formed by connecting the lows of the left and right shoulders. This is considered a strong signal that the trend is about to reverse and that prices will likely head higher or lower, depending on the pattern's direction.

You can use volume indicators, trendlines, or moving averages to confirm the head and shoulders pattern. When the neckline is broken, high volume on the downside can further confirm the pattern and suggest a strong bearish reversal. Traders often use stop-loss orders and profit targets to manage risk and optimize returns when trading this pattern.

Wedges

Wedges are a popular chart pattern used in technical analysis that can signal a reversal in the current trend. They are formed by two converging trendlines which connect the highs and lows of the price action. There are two types of wedges: rising and falling.

Rising Wedge

The rising wedge chart pattern is a technical analysis pattern formed when an asset's price makes higher highs and higher lows while the range of price movement narrows over time.

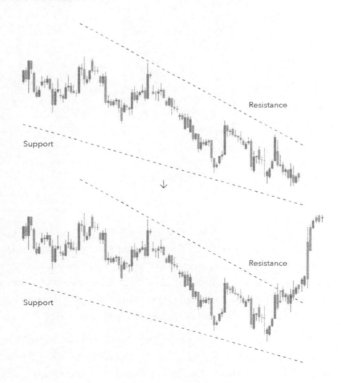

As a result, this creates two converging trendlines, where the upper trendline acts as resistance, and the lower trendline acts as support. The rising wedge is typically seen as a bearish signal, as the narrowing price range indicates that the asset is experiencing weakening momentum, which often leads to a trend reversal.

Traders often look for a break below the lower trendline as a potential sell signal, as this confirms the bearish outlook and signals a possible further decline in price.

Falling Wedge

The falling wedge chart pattern is a technical analysis pattern that can be identified when the price of an asset is making lower highs and lower lows, but the range of price movement narrows over time. This creates two converging trendlines, with the lower trendline acting as support, and the upper trendline acting as resistance. As the trendlines converge, the price will eventually break out of the pattern.

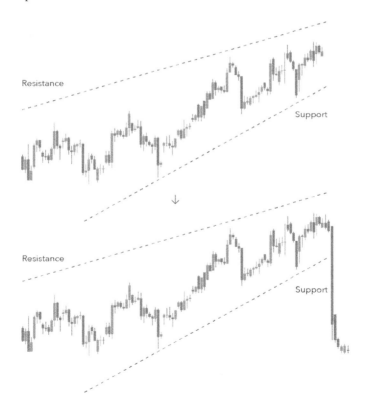

The falling wedge pattern is considered a bullish signal, as it indicates that the asset may be entering a period of consolidation before resuming its upward trend. Conversely, a break above the upper trendline is seen as a potential buy signal, suggesting that the price is breaking out of the pattern and may continue to rise.

Traders can use various indicators to confirm the wedge pattern, including volume indicators and oscillators such as the RSI and MAs. However, when using these indicators, you should look for bullish or bearish signals, such as increasing or decreasing volume or bullish or bearish crossovers of moving averages, to confirm the pattern and potential buy or sell signal.

Flags

The flag chart pattern is a popular technical analysis tool traders use to identify trends in financial markets. The pattern derives its name from the visual resemblance of a flag on a pole. The flag pattern occurs when the price of an asset experiences a strong upward or downward trend and then pauses before continuing in the same direction. The price will move sideways within a relatively narrow range during this pause, often gently oscillating opposite the initial trend.

Pennant

The flag pattern is considered a continuation pattern, suggesting that the initial trend will continue after the pause. Traders often wait for a breakout from the flag pattern before entering a trade. A breakout occurs when the price moves beyond the top or bottom trendline, signaling that the trend is resuming. The flag pattern is useful for traders to identify profitable opportunities in the financial markets.

Bearish Flag Pattern

A bearish flag chart pattern is one type of flag pattern that signals the continuation of a downtrend. This pattern is created when the price of an asset moves down in a strong trend and then pauses sideways to make a flag. The flag is formed by two parallel trendlines, with the upper line acting as resistance and the lower line as support.

After a strong downward move, the price will often consolidate or rebound in a slightly higher consolidation pattern before strongly continuing with the downward trend. This breakout is seen as a sell signal.

Bullish Flag Pattern

The bullish flag chart pattern is formed when the price of an asset is in a strong uptrend and then pauses to consolidate sideways, creating a flag shape before it continues to trend upwards. The flag is formed by two parallel trendlines, with the top trendline acting as resistance and the bottom trendline acting as support.

After a strong move higher, the price will often consolidate or pull back in a sideways pattern, which forms the flag. The consolidation typically occurs on lower trading volume, indicating a pause in the uptrend rather than a reversal. A breakout occurs when the price moves above the resistance level of the flag, which is typically the top trendline.

To confirm the validity of a flag pattern, you should use technical indicators such as moving averages, RSI, Bollinger Bands, Fibonacci retracement, and On Balance Volume (OBV). These indicators can help you identify potential entry and exit points and provide additional insight into a trend's strength.

Cup with Handle

The chart pattern known as the cup with handle is a positive indication in the market and takes the form of a cup and handle, wherein the cup resembles the shape of a "U," and the handle shows a slight decline. It's used to spot opportunities to go long and extend an uptrend.

Cups with longer and more "U" shaped bottoms provide a stronger signal, while cups with sharp "V" bottoms should be treated carefully. Both the cup and the handle should not be overly deep.

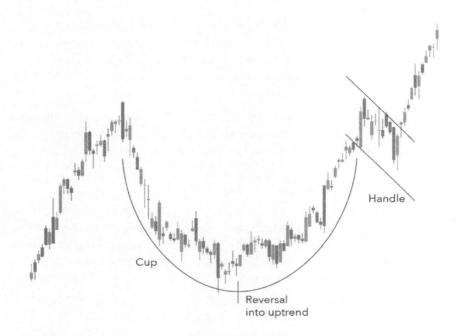

Volume should decrease as prices decline and remain lower than average in the base of the bowl. It should then increase when the stock starts climbing higher, back up to test the previous high.

To confirm the cup with handle pattern, you should use technical indicators such as moving averages, RSI, and OBV.

Rectangles

The rectangle chart pattern is a pattern that suggests that the price of an asset has been fluctuating between two parallel lines of support and resistance, indicating a lack of trend, and is usually seen as a continuation pattern. The price bounces between these two lines, creating a rectangular shape, until it eventually breaks out of the pattern to the upside or downside.

Rectangles can form during both uptrends and downtrends and can last for different durations. The longer the duration of the rectangle, the more significant the pattern is considered to be. The pattern is considered complete when the price breaks out of the rectangle, and a surge in trading volume often accompanies the breakouts.

To trade a rectangle pattern, traders can look for long positions when the price breaks out above the resistance line or short positions when the price breaks below the support line. Traders may also look for a pullback to retest the breakout level before entering a trade.

You can confirm the validity of the rectangle pattern using technical indicators such as moving averages, oscillators like the RSI or stochastic, and volume indicators like OBV.

Triangles

Triangles are a common chart pattern used in technical analysis, which appear as a triangle-like shape. They are similar to wedges and can either be a continuation pattern when validated or can be a powerful reversal pattern in the event of failure. Three types of triangles can develop as price action carves out a holding pattern: ascending, descending, and symmetrical triangles.

Ascending Triangle

An ascending triangle is a bullish chart pattern characterized by horizontal resistance and rising diagonal support levels. It is typically formed when the price is in an uptrend and experiences a period of consolidation. During this consolidation phase, the price oscillates between a horizontal resistance level and a rising diagonal support level, creating a triangular shape.

The pattern is considered bullish because it signals that buyers are gradually becoming more aggressive as the price nears the resistance level. When the price finally breaks out above the resistance level, it is typically accompanied by rising volume as buyers rush in to buy.

The upper trendline must be horizontal and act as a resistance level, while the lower trendline rises diagonally, indicating higher lows. The ascending triangle pattern suggests buyers are gradually gaining momentum as they push prices higher. Once the price breaks out above the resistance level, the upper trendline, formerly a resistance level, becomes support.

Descending Triangle

The descending triangle chart pattern is a bearish formation essentially opposite of the ascending triangle. It typically forms during a downtrend and signals a continuation of the existing trend.

The pattern has a lower horizontal trendline connecting near identical lows, while the upper trendline declines diagonally toward the apex. The pattern gets confirmed when the price breaks through the lower horizontal trendline with strong volume, signaling a downtrend continuation. The lower trendline, formerly a support level, now becomes a resistance level.

Symmetrical Triangle

The symmetrical triangle chart pattern is a technical analysis pattern in which two trendlines converge toward each other, forming a triangle-like shape. The upper trendline slows downward, while the lower trendline slows upward at approximately the same angle until they eventually intersect at the pattern's apex.

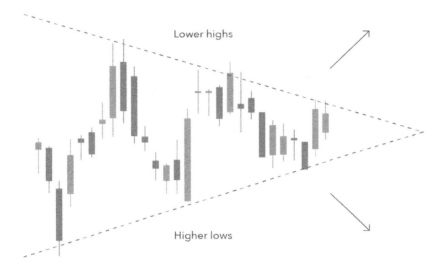

As the price continues to move toward the apex, it will inevitably breach the upper or lower trendline for a breakout. If the price breaks above the upper trendline, it signals an uptrend on rising prices. If it breaks below the lower trendline, it signals a downtrend with falling prices. It is also possible that the price will continue to move within the triangle, in which case traders may wait for a breakout before making a move.

To confirm triangle chart patterns, you may use technical indicators such as moving averages, RSI, Bollinger Bands, Fibonacci retracement levels, and On Balance Volume (OBV). These indicators help you identify potential support and resistance levels and confirm price trends and momentum.

If you have been paying attention so far, you might have noticed I always mention confirming chart patterns with technical indicators. This is because it's an essential part of technical analysis. While chart patterns provide a visual representation of price movements, trend reversals, and continuations, technical indicators help confirm or deny the signals generated by chart patterns. Thankfully, we already covered everything about technical indicators in Chapters 2 and 3, so feel free to refer to them for proper understanding or clarification.

The next chapter will pay attention to the different trading strategies. Knowing these strategies will help you determine what you are good at in trading, how long you're willing to hold positions in the market, which patterns and technical tools work best for you, and so on. Ultimately, having and using a proven strategy that suits your trading lifestyle is all you need to have an advantage over the market.

Key Takeaways

- A chart pattern is a shape that appears on a price chart, which predicts what direction prices might go next by using a series of trendlines or curves.

- While many chart patterns are used in technical analysis, they all fall majorly into two categories: reversal and continuation patterns.

- Reversal chart patterns include double tops and bottoms, head and shoulders, and wedges.

- Continuation patterns include flags, the cup with handle, rectangles, and triangles.

- The longer a continuation and reversal pattern forms, the higher the price movement within it and the more dramatic the expected move once the price breaks out.

Chapter 7

The Trading Edge

"Whatever method you use to enter trades, the most critical thing is that if there is a major trend, your approach should assure that you get in that trend."
— *Richard Dennis*

Emotions are a natural part of trading and can impact your decision-making. For instance, have you ever experienced fear or greed when trading?

New traders often make the mistake of holding onto losing trades, hoping for a turnaround, and exiting winning trades too soon out of fear of losing their profits if the market reverses.

Examining these issues closely, you would discover that they occur because these traders don't have an edge in the market. Thus, regardless of the kind of security you are trading, you must have sound trading strategies.

To succeed in the highly competitive financial markets, you need to adopt thoroughly tested and proven trading strategies. Adopting a trading style based on haphazard cross-trading, where you enter positions on various assets without following a systematic approach, is a recipe for failure. Therefore, it's recommended to have a well-defined trading system in place.

John Paulson is a billionaire hedge fund manager who uses technical analysis religiously. He rose to fame in 2007 in light of the financial crisis. In 2007 alone, after several bets and shorts against the housing market, his hedge firm, Paulson and Co., made $15 billion in profit.

Paulson's profit that year was estimated at $3–4 billion. During the financial crisis, Paulson's bearish view of the credit market went beyond housing and expanded from consumer to corporate debt. Then in 2008, he bet against large financial institutions in the US and the UK, causing many to fail. As expected, harsh criticism followed his actions. And after 2008, his outlook became more bullish.

One of the keys to Paulson's success is his ability to conduct extensive research and analysis to identify undervalued assets and market inefficiencies.

After identifying these, he focuses on finding the right strategy for that asset and using the rules or information to make investment decisions.

By following a set of rules outlined by a trading strategy, you will remove destructive emotions from your trading and eventually have a winning edge in the market. It becomes more easier to open, manage, and stick to profitable trade when you have and understand clear set of rules that define how to manage your profits. Also, closing a losing and non-performing trade will become a normal trading decision if you have a successful strategy.

Momentum Trading

In Chapter 4, I explained briefly what momentum trading is. This section will dive a little deeper. Again, the saying, "the trend is your friend," comes to play here. Momentum traders and investors aim to benefit from either upward or downward trends in a security's price.

Momentum trading involves making money by trading stocks based on current trends. For instance, when a stock's price skyrockets after releasing an impressive earnings report, momentum traders buy shares hoping to increase the stock's price. Alternatively, if a stock's price surges due to rumors of a short squeeze, momentum traders might purchase shares in anticipation of the sharp reduction, thereby pushing the price further.

Traders who use this technique seek to profit from trends that persist in the market, assuming that stocks that have been performing well will likely continue doing so soon. Despite some individuals' aversion to investing in markets reaching new highs, there is significant evidence to suggest that markets that hit new highs tend to keep making higher highs.

When looking at price momentum, traders examine securities rising continuously for days, weeks, or even months. One way to locate momentum stocks is to use a stock screener to filter all of the stocks trading within, for example, 10% of their 52-week highs. Alternatively, traders may prefer to examine the percentage price change over the previous twelve or twenty-four weeks. Generally, the former approach is more sensitive to recent price movements.

In mid-2008, the oil and energy sector served as an example of how it was continuously ranked as one of the top performers based on its twelve-week or twenty-four-week price performance, despite collapsing. This was due to the substantial gains that occurred in the first part of the twelve- or twenty-four-week periods, which obscured any significant decline that followed over many weeks.

To detect trends at an early stage, consider adding a shorter-term price change element, such as a one-week or four-week price change measure. This is beneficial when entering or exiting a specific security.

To become a successful momentum trader, you must quickly and accurately identify the top-performing sectors. Although many screeners are available to use there, you can still use the following fundamental steps to identify such securities:

- First, you must identify the securities you are interested in.

- Count the number of equities trading near their yearly highs.

- Sort the selected securities from highest to lowest to see which performs best.

- Plan an entry: you may wish to enter an instrument while displaying short-term strength, or you may want to wait for a pullback and purchase on weakness. Either technique can work, but whichever one you choose, it's crucial that you follow through with it.

- Plan your exit: going into the trade, you should determine at what moment or under what conditions you will take profits, or you will leave with a loss.

To minimize losses in a momentum trading strategy, it's important to pay attention to volatility, as this type of trading can result in higher volatility than other strategies. To mitigate potential losses, momentum traders typically use stop-loss orders or other risk management techniques.

Momentum trading can be either long-term or short-term. For instance, Tesla (NASDAQ: TSLA) has been a popular momentum stock for years, with its chart consistently showing an upward trend.

Long-term momentum trading is also known as "position trading," while intermediate-term momentum trading is sometimes called "swing trading." Finally, the short-term version of momentum trading is called day trading. So, in essence, momentum trading involves holding positions for a few days to a few weeks.

Momentum trading relies heavily on technical analysis, using indicators such as MAs, RSI, and stochastic oscillators to identify market trends, momentum, and overbought or oversold conditions.

In addition to technical analysis, momentum traders use fundamental analysis to evaluate a company's financial health and market trends. This involves analyzing financial statements, economic data, and news events to gain insight into the underlying factors that may be driving the price movements of a security.

Position Trading

Position trading is a well-known approach that involves keeping a position open for a prolonged period, typically lasting several months or even years. Unlike day traders who focus on short-term price fluctuations, position traders are less concerned with minor price movements and rely heavily on fundamental analysis and long-term trends.

By analyzing a security's underlying fundamentals, position traders can make informed trading decisions and identify when the market aligns with their investment objectives. Once they have confirmed that the price action is consistent with the fundamental shift, they execute their trades. Generally, position traders aim to capture profits from large market movements by holding positions from several months to several years.

Position trading is a strategy involving holding a position for a longer period, usually for months or even years. This style of trading is similar to buy-and-hold investing but with the added benefit of being able to take both long and short positions. Although position trading has greater profit potential, it also involves more risk. Nevertheless, many famous traders, including Joe Ross and Philip A. Fisher, have made fortunes by implementing position trading strategies.

Joe Ross, for instance, once talked about a trader who opened a long position on S&P 500 for almost ten years, from 1991 to 2000. The trader used a trailing stop triggered only when they felt a good profit had been made, resulting in a profit of 16 million dollars.

Another famous position trader, Philip A. Fisher, was an excellent investor who focused on good companies with encouraging data. He invested long-term in Motorola shares in 1955 and held that position until he died at age ninety-six. Fisher was followed by a large crowd of admirers, including Warren Buffet.

Position trading involves trading company shares as they tend to follow stable trends compared to volatile markets such as cryptocurrencies and certain forex markets. Position traders rely on the fundamental analysis of underlying companies to evaluate their true value and identify opportunities for long-term investments. They can also negotiate based on where they think companies or industrial sectors will be in the future.

Breakout trading is a useful strategy for position traders as it can indicate the start of the next significant market movement. This technique allows traders to open a position at the beginning of a trend.

The fifty-day simple moving average is a crucial technical indicator for position traders because it is a factor of 100 and 200, which are accurate indicators of significant long-term trends.

Support and resistance levels can be helpful to traders in determining asset price direction and decide whether to open or close a position. There are short-term and historical support levels that persist for years and resistance levels, which refer to price thresholds that securities have been unable to overcome historically.

Position traders use long-term resistance levels to determine when to close a position, anticipating a drop in security value once it reaches this level. Conversely, they can buy at historical support levels if they expect a long-term upward trend.

Swing Trading

Swing trading is a trading approach that concentrates on earning profits from short- to medium-term price movements by holding positions for a few days to a few weeks while minimizing losses by quickly cutting them. The earnings might be smaller, but with consistent execution over time, they can lead to excellent yearly returns. While swing trading positions usually last a few days to a few weeks, they can also last longer.

This trading strategy uses technical and fundamental analysis to determine market direction and the best entry and exit points. Because there will be several intraday price fluctuations as the trade progresses, patience and composure are required to successfully execute the swing trading strategy.

Furthermore, swing trading is a flexible approach that can be implemented in most markets. Due to the relatively large profit targets, swing traders can also trade assets with wider spreads or lower liquidity.

Swing traders aim for smaller profits than typical stock traders, usually targeting 5% to 10% gains every week or two instead of aiming for 20% to 25%. Although these smaller gains may not seem significant, they can increase over time. Rather than holding positions for weeks or months, swing traders usually hold positions for five to ten days to make small wins, contributing to overall returns.

To achieve growth in your portfolio, you must keep your losses to a minimum. Swing traders aim to take losses quicker than typical traders, with a maximum loss of 3% to 4% rather than the typical 7% to 8%. By keeping losses small, traders can maintain a 3-to-1 profit-to-loss ratio, which is the key to success in portfolio management. In addition, this strategy helps to prevent outsized losses, which could quickly eliminate progress made with smaller gains.

Swing traders can use the Fibonacci retracement tool to identify optimal price entry areas. During a trending market, the price typically retracts before resuming the initial trend. The Fibonacci retracement tool plots horizontal support and resistance levels at key levels such as 23.6%, 38.2%, and 61.8%. When trading equities, investors also pay attention to the 50% level as stocks tend to reverse after retracing 50% from peak levels. Swing traders can determine price levels with attractive risk/reward ratios with the Fibonacci retracement tool.

In addition to Fibonacci, swing traders may also enter buy trades when the price bounces off support areas. When a buy trade is initiated, stops are placed just below the support area, while profit targets are set near the resistance area. Similarly, sell trades may be entered when the price rebounds off the resistance area, with stops placed just above the resistance area and profit targets near the support area. It's important to note that when swing trading off support and resistance levels, these levels may switch roles when the price breaches them. For example, if a support line is broken, it becomes a new level of resistance.

Swing traders can also use moving average crosses to identify opportunities in the market. For example, suppose the five-period moving average crosses below the thirteen-period moving average after a period of waning momentum in an uptrend. In that case, it suggests that a downward swing is underway, and traders can place sell trades.

Swing traders also use continuation and reversal chart patterns to identify potential trades. Wedges and flags are examples of continuation patterns that suggest the asset's price is about to resume its dominant trend after consolidating. In contrast, double tops and head and shoulders are examples of reversal patterns that indicate the momentum of the current trend is fading, and the price is likely to change direction. Candlestick analysis can also help identify swing trading opportunities.

Ultimately, swing trading is a strategy that aims to predict future price movements in the market and capitalize on significant profits when those movements occur. As a result, swing traders use various tactics to achieve their goals.

Day Trading

Nowadays, more and more people are becoming interested in day trading as they seek financial independence and the freedom to live on their terms.

Day trading is a type of trading style that involves buying and selling positions within the same day. Opening and closing a position within a single trading day is considered a day trade. However, if the same position is held overnight and closed the next day, it is no longer considered a day trade.

Day traders usually count on technical analysis to make profits quickly and may use margin to increase their buying power. They aim to make profits by capitalizing on small price movements that occur within the market during a single trading day.

To become successful as a day trader, you must have a refined strategy with specific rules and money management parameters. Day traders look for volatile stocks because it presents an opportunity for profit. Generally, the more a stock moves, the greater the potential profit or loss for a trader.

Risk management is important for day traders as they seek to limit their losses while allowing their winning trades to continue to run. By practicing excellent risk management skills, day traders can protect their capital while earning substantial profits.

Day traders can be considered risk managers as they put their capital at risk to earn profits. However, they may struggle to make consistent profits if they fail to manage their risks effectively.

While there are many strategies for increasing day-trading profits, the following three are particularly crucial:

- **Trade with money you know you can afford to lose:** Setting aside some money for day trading is critical. However, don't trade more than that amount, and don't trade with any of your mortgages or rent money. Why? Because you might misplace it.

- **Start small:** You will make mistakes and lose money day trading, especially in the beginning. So keep a close eye on your losses until you get some experience.

- **Don't quit your day job:** You could have a lucky streak, especially if the market is on a long winning streak. However, before quitting your job and expanding your efforts, you must observe how your trading method performs when the market is volatile, especially during a recession. Then, when you are consistently profitable, you can choose whether you should continue your day job or leave it.

The stock market is a popular choice for day traders due to its size, activity, and relatively low or nonexistent commissions. However, day traders can also trade bonds, options, futures, commodities, and currencies.

When choosing a security to trade, day traders usually look for securities with good volume, as they are liquid and can be bought and sold without significantly affecting the price. Currency markets are also highly liquid. Additionally, securities should have some volatility, but not too much, as volatility is necessary for a day trader to make a profit. Day traders should also know how the security trades and what triggers its movements, such as earnings reports or trading ranges. Following the news can help create volatility and liquidity and provide ideas for trading.

To succeed in day trading, you want to learn to use various technical analysis tools such as moving averages, Fibonacci retracements, and chart patterns to identify potential trade opportunities. For example, you may want to use a fifty-day moving average to determine the overall trend of a stock and a twenty-day moving average to identify potential entry and exit points.

Fibonacci retracements identify potential price levels where security may experience support or resistance. The most commonly used levels are 38.2%, 50%, and 61.8%. You can use these retracement levels as potential entry and exit points.

Chart patterns are also used to identify possible trend reversals or continuation patterns. You can use various chart patterns, such as triangles, head, and shoulders, or double top and bottom, to identify potential trade opportunities. For example, you may use a bullish flag pattern to identify a possible long trade or an inverse head and shoulders pattern to identify a potential short trade.

Again, it's important to reiterate that day trading can be risky and that no trading strategy is foolproof. So, as a day trader, you must have a solid understanding of technical analysis tools and risk management strategies before implementing a day trading strategy. It is also important to have a disciplined approach to trading, including a trading plan and the ability to stick to it, to minimize emotional decision-making and maximize potential profits.

Scalping

Scalping, also called scalp trading, involves short intervals between opening and closing a trade. This trading strategy can be compared to action-packed thriller movies full of suspense and excitement. It is a high-speed and adrenaline-pumping style of trading that can be overwhelming.

Scalp trades are generally closed out within a few seconds to a few minutes at the maximum. The ultimate goal for scalpers is to profit from small price movements in the market over a very short time frame, often just a few seconds or minutes.

Scalping is a trading strategy that demands expertise and a disciplined approach to risk management. If you enjoy fast-paced trading and excitement, lack the patience to wait for extended trades, and can devote several hours to monitoring charts, then scalping might be an ideal approach. However, you must know how to think quickly and adjust direction based on market movements to succeed as a scalper.

On the other hand, if fast-moving environments easily stress you and you can only dedicate a few hours to monitoring charts, then scalping may not suit you.

Therefore, if you prefer taking your time to analyze the market's overall picture and executing fewer trades with higher profit potential, then scalping is probably not for you, and you might want to explore swing trading instead.

Identifying trends, anticipating market movements, and understanding market psychology are crucial to effectively executing the scalping strategy. Effective scalpers should also be skilled in reading and interpreting short-term charts, making decisions based on stock charting within short intervals. Key indicators such as moving averages and Fibonacci retracement levels are important for scalpers to determine if they can execute a trade. Although scalpers often experience losing trades, a successful scalping strategy and discipline can help them maximize wins and minimize losses.

Scalping contradicts the traditional approach of holding onto rallying stocks, at least in short/medium term. Instead, scalpers sell their positions even if the stock is experiencing a large uptick. They may re-enter the security later but have the discipline to exit a stock even if they are making significant gains. In contrast, traditional day traders tend to hold onto the stock, believing it will continue to rise.

Ultimately, you should understand that all of these trading strategies come with significant risk. In essence, you're deciding to invest in a security based on recent activity by other market participants.

Also, remember that the market can always move unexpectedly, and there is no assurance that it will continue in a predicted direction. Unforeseen events, such as a significant news release, can impact how the market is perceived by investors, leading to selling. Additionally, if many investors already have a long position in a security, they may start taking profits, which could outweigh new buyers entering the market, resulting in a price decline.

Therefore, you must learn to risk your money wisely in the market. Aside from having sound trading strategies to attack the market with, you also want an excellent system that serves as a defensive mechanism for managing your money effectively. The next chapter will cover more about this.

Key Takeaways

- Momentum trading involves making money by trading stocks based on current trends.

- Position trading is a strategy involving holding a position for a longer period, usually months or even years.

- Swing trading uses technical and fundamental analysis to determine market direction and the best entry and exit points.

- Day trading is a type of trading style that pertains to buying and selling positions within the same day.

- Scalping, also called scalp trading, is a trading approach involving short intervals between opening and closing a trade.

"The individual investor should act consistently as an investor and not as a speculator."
— Ben Graham

Effective risk management is crucial in the world of trading as it requires traders to possess a comprehensive understanding of the process of identifying, assessing, and controlling potential risks.

For instance, let's say you take a trade after identifying a stock that you believe is undervalued and poised for a rebound. Then, you decide to buy a large position in the stock, using leverage to amplify your potential gains.

Unfortunately, the trade does not go as planned, and the stock price continues to decline. At one point, you are down over $14,000, which is a significant sum of money for you. However, instead of panicking and holding on to the position, hoping for a rebound, you cut your losses quickly and get out of the trade.

Your decision to exit the trade might be right if the stock continues to decline in price, and you would have lost even more money if you had held on.

In essence, I'm saying that by being disciplined and managing your risk, you can avoid a catastrophic loss and live to trade another day.

Martin Schwartz, also known as "Buzzy," is another successful trader who has made millions in the markets by using technical analysis to identify market trends and make profitable trades.

In his first year as an independent stock trader, he earned $600,000, which he doubled the next year. Schwartz claimed that he used to make approximately $70,000 daily through trading and even made several million dollars in a day. However, as his obsessive trading started to dominate his life, a health issue prompted him to take a step back, and he has since lived a semi-retired life, engaging only in reduced-scale trading from his home in Florida.

Today, Schwartz's keen focus on risk management sets him apart from other traders. He now believes that a trader should have a well-defined risk management plan and a proven trading plan that is based on sound rules, such as only taking trades where the potential reward outweighs the risk, cutting losses quickly when a trade goes against them, and never risking more than a minor percentage of their account on any one trade.

This final chapter examines the importance of protecting your capital by following a few simple risk management rules. That way, you get to stay in the game for the long haul.

Manage Your Risk

Trading involves risk, and it can potentially yield high rewards. In other words, the greater the potential reward, the greater the risk involved. This is particularly evident when using leveraged products. Using leverage refers to not putting up the entire value of the trade when opening or holding a position but rather only a small portion of it, called margin.

If we take Gold as an example and say, it requires a margin of 6%, which means you only need to put forward 6% of the total trade value to open the position. However, profits and losses are based on the full size of the trade. Therefore, leveraging a small deposit can result in significant gains or losses. Consequently, it is crucial to manage your losses effectively to avoid depleting your account rapidly.

Effective risk management is one of the essential components of trading, alongside trading strategy and psychology. Even if a trader has a superior trading strategy and impeccable psychological control, their account could quickly be decimated without a robust risk management plan to limit losses on unsuccessful trades. Moreover, since winning every trade is impossible, managing risk carefully is crucial.

Risk management refers to the processes put into place when trading to help keep losses under control and a good risk/reward ratio. With the right application of risk management, you can cut down on your losses and maximize your profits. It makes no difference if you are a beginner or an experienced trader. You must learn to apply risk management when trading the financial market.

Tips for Good Risk Management

As I explained earlier, limiting your losses is crucial because even the most skilled traders will eventually experience losses. But by managing your risks and keeping losses manageable, you will increase the likelihood of staying in the market for longer and achieving more successful trades. Below, I have shared the different tips I have used to have a winning edge in the market over the years:

Stick to Your Trading Plan

A trading strategy with a risk management component is essential to prevent traders from making impulsive decisions based on emotions rather than their outlined strategy. A good plan or strategy is only effective if followed, and emotions can easily hinder this. Therefore, having a clear trading strategy that outlines the conditions for entering, managing, and exiting trades is crucial.

Strictly following a plan is fundamental to a successful trading approach, as it helps eliminate unnecessary emotional and psychological influences, which is why a risk management strategy is vital.

Maintain a Good Risk-Reward Ratio

The risk-reward ratio is a computation that compares the probable loss from a trade (the risk) to the expected potential return (the reward).

$$\frac{Risk}{Reward} = \frac{Potential\ loss}{Potential\ profit}$$

So, if you bought Gold at $1,980 with a target to take profit at $2,010, and placed your stop-loss at $1970, then your risk-reward ratio would be as follows:

= (1,980 − 1,970) / (2,010 − 1,970)

= 10 / 40

= 1:4

Generally, you should try to join trades with a risk-reward ratio greater than 1:1, with the aim of making at least as much as you risk. Ideally, every trade should have a risk-reward ratio greater than 1:2.

Now, to determine exactly how much you're willing to risk or lose on a trade, you'll have to learn to determine the right position size. We'll discuss that in the next section.

Risk Only What You're Prepared to Lose

Many traders, including experienced ones, make a major error of trading with a position size that is too large. For instance, let's say you have $10,000 in your account and open a leveraged trade worth $179,800. Assuming a margin requirement for an S&P 500 trade is 5%. This means that you must have 5% of $179,800 in your account to open the trade (not including trading costs).

5% x $179,800 = $8,990.

So, if you have $10,000 in your account and open a leveraged trade worth $187,500 with a margin requirement of 5%, you need $9,375 in your account to open the trade. This leaves very little room for the trade to move before your available funds are used up, resulting in the position being closed due to the margin closeout policy.

Now let's consider another example.

Let's say, this time, you have $10,000 in your account and open a position on Bitcoin valued at $30,500. The margin requirement is $1,875.

If you have $10,000 in your account and use $1,875 as margin, you are giving your trade more room to grow and can pick where to place your stop loss rather than having the trade closed out due to the margin closeout rules.

Successful traders aim to risk at most 1–2% of their account on any trade, which means risking $100 to $200 per trade if you have $10,000 in your trading account.

Taking small risks reduces the likelihood of losing your account with one or two losing trades. However, taking more significant risks can be dangerous and harmful to your long-term profitability. As a competent market strategist, it is essential to be disciplined and remain objective with the numbers.

Always use a Stop Loss

One of the crucial rules to follow in trading is using stop-loss orders. These orders instruct your broker to buy or sell a market when it reaches a predetermined price that you have set. For example, if you purchased an asset for $240 and wanted to limit your potential loss to $20, you would place a stop-loss order at $220. Then, if the asset's price drops and reaches or goes below $220, the trade will automatically close, locking your loss at $20.

Setting a stop-loss order is crucial to sticking to a trading strategy and calculating the risk-reward ratio, both of which are essential to any risk management approach. However, it's not sufficient to merely set a stop-loss order; it's vital to keep to it. Moving it away when the market moves toward it will only increase your potential loss, defeating the purpose of using a stop-loss order.

Protect Your Profits With Trailing Stops

In addition to implementing stop-losses to minimize losses, you can also employ trailing stops to safeguard your profits. A trailing stop is a stop order that trails behind the current market price as it moves in your favor. It adjusts automatically to the changes in market price and follows along at a set distance, either below the current market price if you are long or above it if you are short.

For example, if you buy an asset at $120.00 and set an initial trailing stop at $110.00 with a trailing amount of $10.00, your stop-loss order will be adjusted automatically to $111.00 if the stock price increases by $1.00 to $121.00. Conversely, if the stock price declines, your stop-loss order will remain at $110.00 for a stop-loss of $10.00.

Trailing stops are an effective tool to lock in profits as the market price moves in your favor while protecting against downside risk. However, it is important to understand that the trailing stop does not guarantee that your position will be sold at the trailing amount. Rather, it's simply a limit order that will only execute at or better than the trailing amount.

Deal With Fear and Greed

Overcoming fear and greed is a crucial challenge that traders face when trading in the financial markets. Fear can lead traders to hesitate or make impulsive decisions, while greed can drive traders to take excessive risks or hold onto positions for too long. However, successful traders often develop strategies to manage these emotions and maintain a disciplined approach to trading. This may involve setting clear goals, establishing risk management plans, and maintaining a rational mindset.

Practice Hedging

Hedging is a risk management technique in equities involving derivative instruments like Futures and Options contracts. These contracts allow you to lock in a price for a future transaction, reducing the risk of price fluctuations. For example, with a Futures contract, you can agree on a fixed price for a future buy or sell transaction. This way, even if the price of your asset falls, you can still sell it at the higher price you fixed.

Similarly, thanks to these contracts, you can buy at lower rates even if the price rises. Different types of derivative contracts are available for hedging, and you can learn more about them online.

Diversify Your Portfolio

Diversifying your investments by spreading your capital across multiple assets is essential to protect your portfolio from uncertainties that can lead to significant losses. In addition, this approach helps minimize the impact of underperforming stocks on your overall portfolio.

However, it's important to diversify across stocks with minimal correlation, as investing in similar stocks will expose you to similar risks, defeating the purpose of diversification. For instance, there may be better approaches than investing in both the automobile and auto ancillary sectors since they are affected by similar factors.

Diversification doesn't necessarily mean investing equally across all sectors but in multiple assets or sectors. You may choose to invest more in companies you are optimistic about, but it is important to invest within your risk tolerance level to avoid incurring significant losses.

The Dos and Don'ts of Trading

So, I want us to wrap up by looking at the biggest dos and don'ts to pay detailed attention to when trading the financial markets. Bear in mind that following the points covered below can help you stay on the right track with your trading:

The Dos

1. **Educate yourself on the markets, the securities you're trading, and different trading strategies.**

    Understanding the financial markets and the securities you are trading is essential to becoming a successful trader. However, this requires continuous learning and keeping up with current trends and events affecting the markets. Additionally, it's important to have a comprehensive understanding of different trading strategies, such as technical and fundamental analysis, to make informed decisions.

2. **Use a trading plan with clear goals and risk management strategies.**

    An important part of trading is having a well-defined trading plan that outlines your goals and objectives. Your trading plan should also include risk management strategies capable of helping you minimize losses and protect your capital. Risk management strategies include setting stop-loss orders, managing position size, and diversifying your portfolio.

3. **Practice discipline and patience, especially when sticking to your trading plan and avoiding impulsive decisions.**

   Discipline and patience are critical in trading, and traders must remain calm and focused on their trading plan. Traders should also avoid making impulsive decisions and chasing trades that do not meet their criteria. Emotions like fear and greed can be detrimental to trading success, and traders must learn to control them.

4. **Maintain a diverse portfolio to spread out risk.**

   We discussed diversification earlier; practicing it is essential in trading as it helps spread risk and minimize potential losses. Maintaining a diversified portfolio means investing in different asset classes, such as commodities, stocks, cryptocurrency, and various sectors of the economy. By diversifying their investments, traders can reduce their exposure to any security or sector.

5. **Monitor market news and trends to stay current on potential opportunities and risks.**

   Traders must stay informed about market news and trends to identify potential opportunities and risks. Keeping up with economic indicators, earnings reports, and other news events can help traders make informed trading decisions.

The Don'ts

1. **Avoid trading with money you can't afford to lose.**

   This fundamental principle of investing is especially relevant when it comes to trading. While making money in the markets is always possible, there are no guarantees, so you must be prepared for the possibility of losses. Therefore, it is usually recommended that you only invest an amount of money you know you can afford to lose and keep your trading capital separate from your day-to-day living expenses.

2. **Don't let emotions drive your trading decisions.**

   Emotions such as fear, greed, and overconfidence can all lead to costly mistakes in trading. For instance, fear can cause you to exit a trade too early, while greed can lead to over-trading or holding onto positions for too long. Likewise, overconfidence can make you underestimate the risks involved in a particular trade. So, it is important that you always remain calm and rational and stick to your trading plan and risk management strategies.

3. **Never chase losses or over-trade to make up for losses.**

   Losing money in a trade can be a frustrating experience, but it is important to avoid being tempted to try to make up for those losses by taking bigger risks or trading more frequently. This common mistake can lead to even bigger losses. So, rather than giving in to that temptation, accept losses as a normal part of trading and move on to the next opportunity.

4. **Don't neglect risk management strategies.**

   Risk management is an important part of trading, and several methods can help you manage risk effectively. These include using stop-loss orders to limit losses, hedging techniques to protect against market volatility, and diversifying risk across different assets. Therefore, it is crucial that you put a clear risk management plan in place before you begin to trade.

5. **Don't ignore fees and commissions.**

   Fees and commissions can take a chunk out of your profits quickly, especially if you make frequent trades or trade with a small account balance. Therefore, it is important to know the fees associated with different trading platforms and instruments and to make allowances for these costs in your trading plan.

6. **Avoid trying to time the market.**

   Timing the market can be difficult, even for experienced traders. Attempting to predict the future direction of the markets can lead to impulsive decisions and distract you from your trading plan. Instead, focus on identifying opportunities based on market trends and your analysis, and be prepared to adjust your trading strategy as market conditions change.

Looking at all that we've covered in this chapter, the vast majority of the rules outlined have a thing in common: they aim to manage risk and minimize losses to make money in the financial markets. Of course, losses will inevitably occur, but successful traders keep them small to continue to trade and identify profitable opportunities.

Experienced traders understand when to cut their losses and have incorporated this strategy into their overall approach. Additionally, they know when it is appropriate to take profits by either moving their stop loss to secure some gains or exiting the trade entirely. In any case, traders should remember that there will always be new opportunities to trade in the future.

Key Takeaways

- Trading involves risk and can yield high rewards. In other words, the greater the potential reward, the greater the risk involved.

- By managing your risks and losses, you will increase the likelihood of staying in the market for longer and achieving more successful trades.

- A trading plan should also include risk management strategies that help you minimize losses and protect your capital.

- Setting a stop-loss order is crucial to sticking to a trading strategy and calculating the risk-reward ratio, both of which are essential to any risk management approach.

CONCLUSION

"The hard work in trading comes in the preparation. The actual process of trading, however, should be effortless."
— Jack Schwager

Congratulations on taking the most important first step that so many fail to take.

As you can see, technical analysis is a powerful tool that you can use to make informed decisions about a wide range of securities, including stocks, bonds, commodities, and currencies. By studying charts and identifying patterns and trends, you can predict future price movements and exploit profitable opportunities.

You do not need to have or use fancy mathematical equations as an analyst or trader. However, from all we've covered, you can see that it is still possible to analyze a market using simple open, high, low, and close data of the candlesticks. Once you understand the basic tools you need to analyze a market, the rest is up to study and experimentation.

Over the years, I've seen people build life-changing generational wealth from the financial market. But I've also seen countless people lose the money they made from the market twice as fast.

I have survived only because of my dedication to learning and understanding market trends and patterns. This has enabled me to make profitable trades and achieve impressive investment returns consistently.

Through years of experience, I've honed my swing trader skills and developed a strategic approach to trading that emphasizes risk management and discipline. As a result, I can easily identify key support and resistance levels and also utilize technical indicators to confirm trends and capitalize on market volatility.

Despite facing many challenges in the market, including unpredictable price fluctuations and unexpected news events, I've remained steadfast in my approach and have continued to succeed. My commitment to learning and adapting to changing market conditions has been a key factor in my success.

At this point, you might wonder, *how long will it take me to become a profitable trader?*

While some individuals with talent may become profitable in three to six months, it could take others several years.

Nonetheless, the journey is truly worthwhile if you stick to it. Therefore, it's essential to be ready for multiple failures and not be rushed.

Always remember the market is moving either as an uptrend, downtrend, or range horizontally. So, learn how to use the tools we discussed to analyze these market conditions. Always know the current trend and look for candlesticks and chart patterns to help you decide when to enter and exit a trade.

Whether you're a seasoned trader or you are a beginner, it's your responsibility to hone your technical analysis skills and maximize your profits. So, continually educate yourself and stay current on new market developments and changes. By constantly adapting and improving one's skills and strategies, you can better navigate the complexities of the markets and increase your chances of success.

However, remember that technical analysis is just one approach and should be used with other forms of analysis, such as fundamental analysis and market sentiment analysis, to make investment decisions.

Finally, if you enjoyed reading this book, it would mean a lot to me if you could leave a review with your feedback.

If you're still reading to the end, I appreciate you—best of luck on your trading and investing journey.

To your success,

Brian Hale

REFERENCES

Abhishek, K. (2023, Mar 31). 21 Do's and Don'ts of Stock Market Investing for Beginners. Trade Brains. https://tradebrains.in/dos-and-donts-of-stock-market-investing.

AVATrade. (2023). Swing Trading. https://www.avatrade.co.za/education/trading-for-beginners/swing-trading.

CFI Team. (2023, March 21). Scalping (Day Trading Technique). Corporate Finance Institute. https://corporatefinanceinstitute.com/resources/wealth-management/scalping-day-trading-technique.

CFI Team. (2023, April 2). Stochastic Oscillator. Corporate Finance Institute. https://corporatefinanceinstitute.com/resources/capital-markets/stochastic-oscillator.

CenterPoint Securities. (2023). The Ultimate Guide to Trendlines. https://centerpointsecurities.com/trendlines.

Chand, S. (2023). What are the Limitations of Charts in Technical Analysis? YourArticleLibrary. https://www.yourarticlelibrary.com/investment/what-are-the-limitations-of-charts-in-technical-analysis/1770.

Chen, J. (2021, September 29). Technical Indicator: Definition, Analyst Uses, Types and Examples. Investopedia. https://www.investopedia.com/terms/t/technicalindica.

Cintolo, M. (2022, December 29). Why Is Trading Volume So Important? Cabot Wealth Network. https://www.cabotwealth.com/daily/stock-market/trading-volume-important.

Cliffe, C. (2023). 10 chart patterns every trader needs to know. IG. https://www.ig.com/za/trading-strategies/10-chart-patterns-every-trader-needs-to-know-190514#Cup_and_handle.

CMC Markets. (2023). Position trading. https://www.cmcmarkets.com/en/trading-guides/position-trading#:~:text.

CMC Markets. (2023). How to trade with Fibonacci. https://www.cmcmarkets.com/en/trading-guides/how-to-trade-with-fibonacci.

Daniels Trading. (2022, April 26). Technical Analysis of Stocks: Understand the Pros and Cons. https://www.danielstrading.com/2022/04/26.

Dennis, R. (2022, July 17). The Turtle Trader – Trend Following And Trading Strategies. Quantified Strategies. https://www.quantifiedstrategies.com/richard-dennis/#Quotes_from_Richard_Dennis.

eToro. (2018, November 21). The trend is your friend: an easy guide to trend trading. https://www.etoro.com/news-and-analysis/etoro-updates/the-trend-is-your-friend-an-easy-guide-to-trend-trading.

Elearnmarkets. (2022, July 13). All 35 Candlestick Chart Patterns in the Stock Market-Explained. https://www.elearnmarkets.com/blog/35-candlestick-patterns-in-stock-market.

Frankel, M. (2022, Jul 11). What Is Momentum Trading? The Motley Fool. https://www.fool.com/investing/stock-market/types-of-stocks/momentum-stocks/momentum-trading.

Genesis Vision. (2018, Dec 12). The Rice Origins of the Candlestick. https://blog.genesis.vision/the-rice-origins-of-the-candlestick-2d889cb22e21.

Gilmartin Group. (2023). Why Does Trading Volume Matter? https://gilmartinir.com/why-does-trading-volume-matter.

Hayes, A. (2022, July 08). On-Balance Volume (OBV): Definition, Formula, and Uses as Indicator. Investopedia. https://www.investopedia.com/terms/o/onbalancevolume.asp.

iBillionaire Capital. (2015, Jun 3). Billionaire Bio: John Paulson's Impressive Road to Success. Medium. https://medium.com/ibillionaire/billionaire-bio-john-paulsons-impressive-road-to-success-bfd3c786d360.

Investor's Business Daily. (2023). What's in a Stock Chart? https://www.investors.com/ibd-university/chart-reading/chart-contents,

Lawler, J. (2020, September 2). What is trading risk management? FlowBank. https://www.flowbank.com/en/research/what-is-trading-risk-management.

Learntotrade. (2018, May 11). The Biggest Do's & Don'ts of Trading. Learn To Trade. https://www.learntotrade.com.au/blog/monthly-market-reports/the-biggest-dos-donts-of-trading.

Lemo, A. (2022, April 13). Bollinger Bands Trading Strategy & Period Setting. Daily Forex. https://www.dailyforex.com/forex-articles/2009/09/forex-trading-and-bollinger-bands/22173.

Loo, A. (2023, February 19). Technical Analysis – A Beginner's Guide. Corporate Finance Institute. https://corporatefinanceinstitute.com/resources/capital-markets/technical-analysis.

Market Volume. (2023). Volume RSI (Relative Strength Index). https://www.marketvolume.com/technicalanalysis/volumersi.asp.

Mehta, V. (2023). Indicators in Stock Markets. MyEspresso. https://www.myespresso.com/bootcamp/module/technical-analysis-indicators-patterns/indicators-in-stock-markets

Miley, S. (2022, June 6). The Trading Risk Management Strategy: Best Tips and Tools. HFTrading. https://hmarkets.com/trading-risk-management-strategy.

Mitchell, C. (2021, May 05). Jesse Livermore: Lessons From a Legendary Trader. Investopedia. https://www.investopedia.com/articles/trading/09/legendary-trader-jesse-livermore.asp.

Motilal Oswal. (2023). What is the Significance of Stock Chart Technical Analysis? https://www.motilaloswal.com/blog-details/what-is-the-significance-of-stock-chart-technical-analysis-/20020.

NirmalBang. (2023). How To Do Trend Analysis? https://www.nirmalbang.com/knowledge-center/trend-analysis.html.

Paluteder, D. (2022, Oct 27). What are Chart Patterns? | Types & Examples | Technical Analysis Guide. Finbold. https://finbold.com/guide/chart-patterns/

Pasi, S. (2023). Multi Timeframe Trading. https://www.myespresso.com/bootcamp/module/trading-styles/multi-timeframe-trading.

Rain Editorial Team. (2022, July 25). Moving Average Technical Indicators Explained. Rain. https://www.rain.com/learn/moving-average-technical-indicators-explained.

Snow, R. (2019, April 24). A Guide to Support and Resistance Trading. DailyFX. https://www.dailyfx.com/education/learn-technical-analysis/support-and-resistance-trading.html.

Stocksharp. (2023). Advantages and Disadvantages of Technical Analysis. https://stocksharp.com/topic/24097/advantages-and-disadvantages-of-technical-analysis.

Tata India. (2023). Welcome to The ATA India Learn Technical analysis. https://tataindia.org/anatomy-of-a-candlestick.

Thakar, C. (2020, Nov 26). Introduction to Risk Management in Trading. QuantInsti. https://blog.quantinsti.com/trading-risk-management.

Thakur, M. (2023). Important Use Of Technical Analysis Indicator (informative). eduCBA. https://www.educba.com/technical-analysis-indicator.

The Editors of Encyclopedia Britannica. (2023, Mar 28). Warren Buffett: American businessman and philanthropist. Encyclopedia Britannica. https://www.britannica.com/biography/Warren-Edward-Buffett.

TheStreet Staff. (2022, October 11). What Is Trading Volume? Definition & Importance. TheStreet. https://www.thestreet.com/dictionary/t/trading-volume.

Trading Strategy Guides. (2017, December 3). Trend Line Trading: The Trend Breaker Strategy. https://tradingstrategyguides.com/trend-line-trading.

Tudor Jones, P. (2022, November 30). Maverick Trader (Quotes And Trading Strategies). Quantified Strategies. https://www.quantifiedstrategies.com/paul-tudor-jones.

Value of Stocks. (2021, December 19). What Is the Meaning Behind "The Trend Is Your Friend"? https://valueofstocks.com/2021/12/19/what-is-the-meaning-behind-the-trend-is-your-friend.

Wallstreetmojo Team. (2023). Average True Range. https://www.wallstreetmojo.com/average-true-range.

Warrior Trading. (2023). Day Trading Guide for Getting Started. https://www.warriortrading.com/day-trading.

Williams, C. (2022, June 28). What Is Trend Analysis? The Balance Money. https://www.thebalancemoney.com/what-is-trend-analysis-5218907.

XGLOBAL MARKETS Blog. (2023). Support and Resistance Lines. https://www.xglobalmarkets.com/learn_center/support-and-resistance.